Strippers in Slippers

A Quiet Reflection of Strippings Past,

a perspective, vague, and abbreviated memoir.

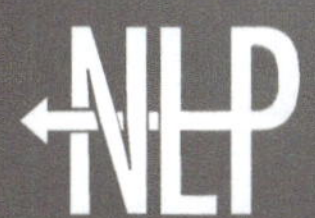

Strippers in Slippers: A Quiet Reflection on Strippings Past

Copyright © 2020 N.P. Anne. Edition & arrangement © Next Left Press.
All rights reserved.

Published by Next Left Press, New Orleans, LA
www.nextleftpress.com

Cover photography: Shadow Angelina Starkey
Design: Geoff Munsterman & N.P. Anna

ISBN-13: 978-0-9962374-7-5

Printed in the United States of America.

Title: Strippers in Slippers / by N.P. Anne.
Description: New Orleans, LA : Next Left Press, 2020. |
ISBN 9780996237475 (pbk.)
Subjects: Exotic Dancing. | Sex work. | Memoir.

This is for the sake of the memory of every single one of you I have ever been fortunate enough to know.

GOOD FOR
ONE FREE DRINK

1000's

Neurosurgeon, TV writer, ER nurse, translator, politician, teacher, Olympian.

If I asked you what all of these things have in common, I feel I can confidently say that exotic dancing would be pretty low on the list. And yet, I personally know at least one person in every one of those fields for whom stripping was part of the journey.

That's the thing, it's a world you cannot understand from the outside, it's a world where every negative stereotype is true, but not for everyone.

You see, there's a difference between stripper as a job title and stripper as a lifestyle choice, and you can't explain it to anyone outside the world. So all these incredibly beautiful strong intelligent warrior women I've known are lumped in and overwhelmed by the stereotypes. Which sucks.

It's a hard job no matter what, harder than you can imagine regardless and only made more painful by people's assumptions and prejudice, to the point that in extreme cases we as dancers are viewed as so subhuman than the most violent and degrading behavior is considered acceptable.

The point I'm taking forever to get to is that in that darkness there are lights, there are fierce beautiful women who will take your hand and drag you out of the nightmare and remind you that they're wrong, that regardless, you are still human, still have value.

For a time, because I am oh so lucky, for me she was that warrior, I am forever changed by the kindness she showed me and the strength she taught me. So listen to her stories, they're all true, try to gain an understanding of something you don't understand.

Who knows? Maybe she will make you a better human being, it worked for me.

—Echo Rhiannon Luben

On Beauty

SPENT THE NIGHT GOING AN HOUR IN THE OPPOSITE DIRECTION. SHOW UP, DRESS, AUDITION. ONE OF THE GIRLS WHO GOT FIRED FROM A FEW PREVIOUS CLUBS I'D WORKED AT COMES AND TELLS ME I LOOK GREAT. AT THIS POINT, I'D LOST 75 LBS. AT MY HEAVIEST AND AT ANOTHER CLUB BY THE SAME NAME 30 MINUTES AWAY I HAD ONCE FOUGHT THAT SAME GIRL'S SISTER.

THE SAME GIRL MONTHS LATER WENT ON ANOTHER AUDITION WITH ME TO A CORPORATE CLUB FURTHER AWAY, MANAGEMENT TELLS ME NOT TO CONTINUE DRESSING. I'M TOO FAT… I LOSE MY WALLET AND MY APPETITE THAT EVENING, BUT I DO FIND MY OLD EATING DISORDER ON THE WAY HOME.

MY FIRST WEEK, THERE WAS A GIRL NAMED MARIA. AS A BABY STRIPPER I'D WATCH HER EVERY MOVE. SHE WAS BEAUTIFUL EXTENSIONS, MAKEUP, NAILS. AND SHE SOLD DANCES; TO THE POINT WHERE EVERYONE, GIRLS AND MANAGEMENT, EVERYWHERE KNEW HER.

I'D TELL HER HOW BEAUTIFUL SHE WAS AND SHE _HATED_ ME FOR IT—WOULD SCREAM AT ME TO SHUT UP.

I GET THAT NOW AND I UNDERSTAND HER.

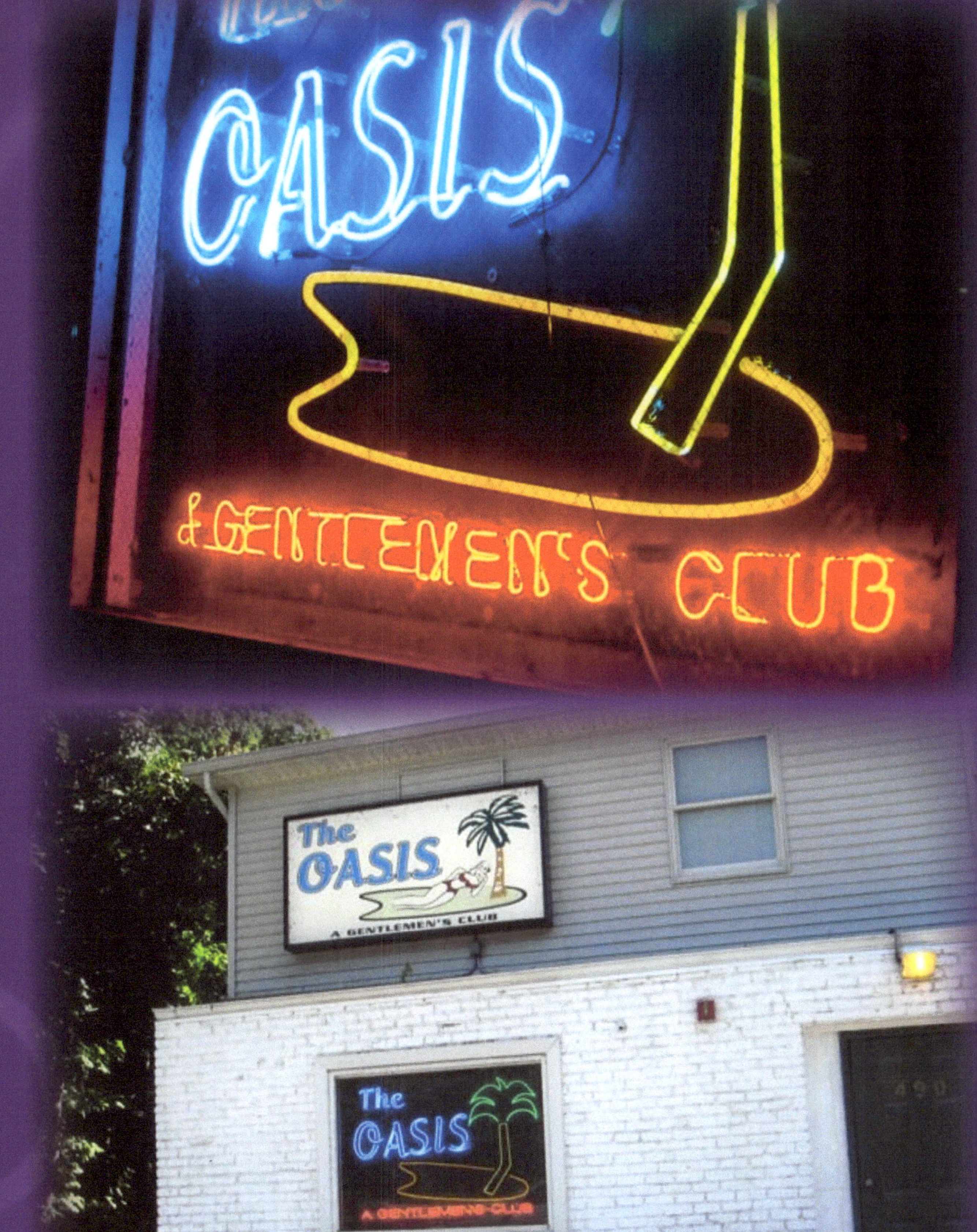
OASIS
& GENTLEMEN'S CLUB
The OASIS
A GENTLEMEN'S CLUB
The OASIS
A GENTLEMEN'S CLUB

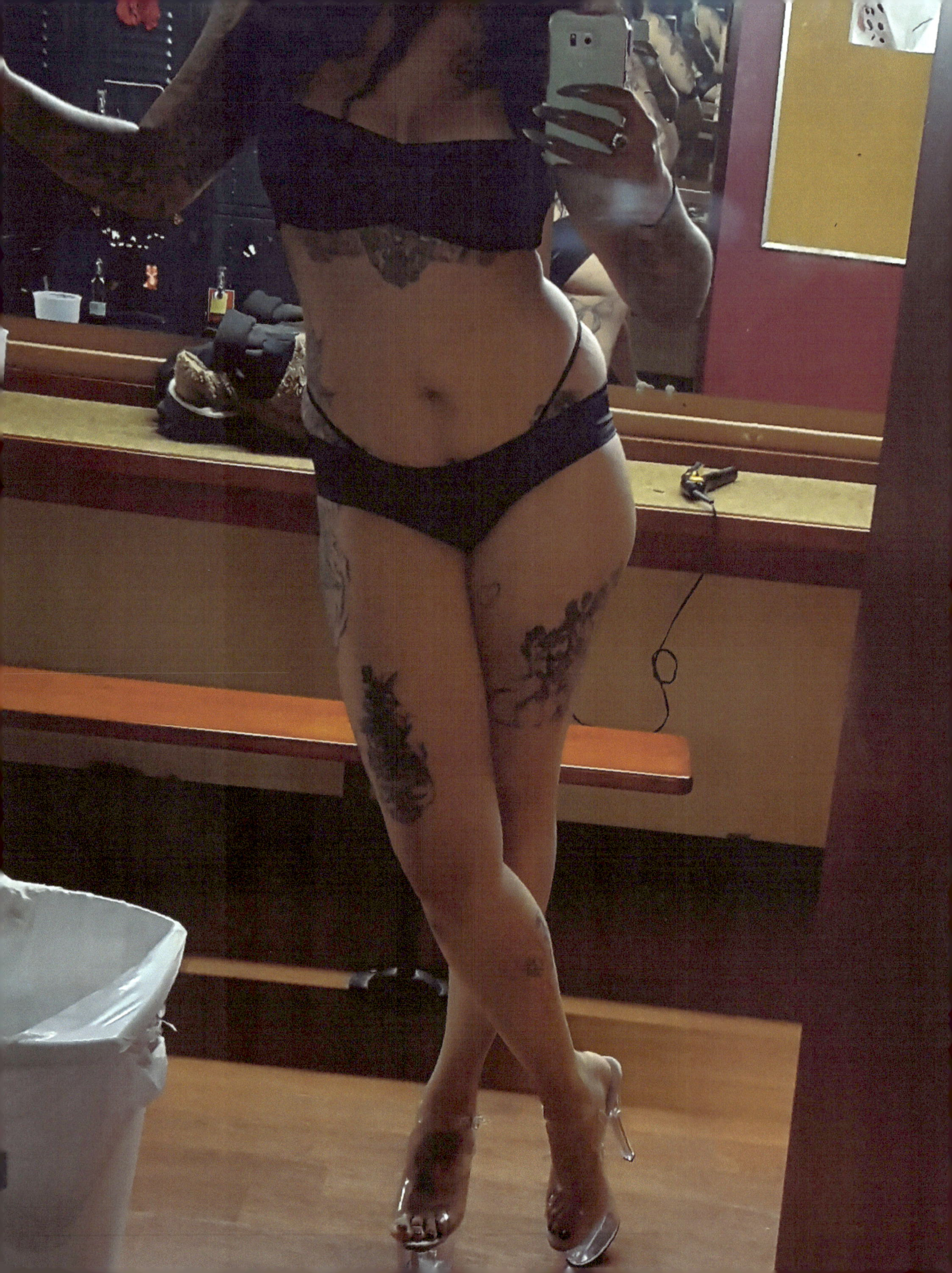

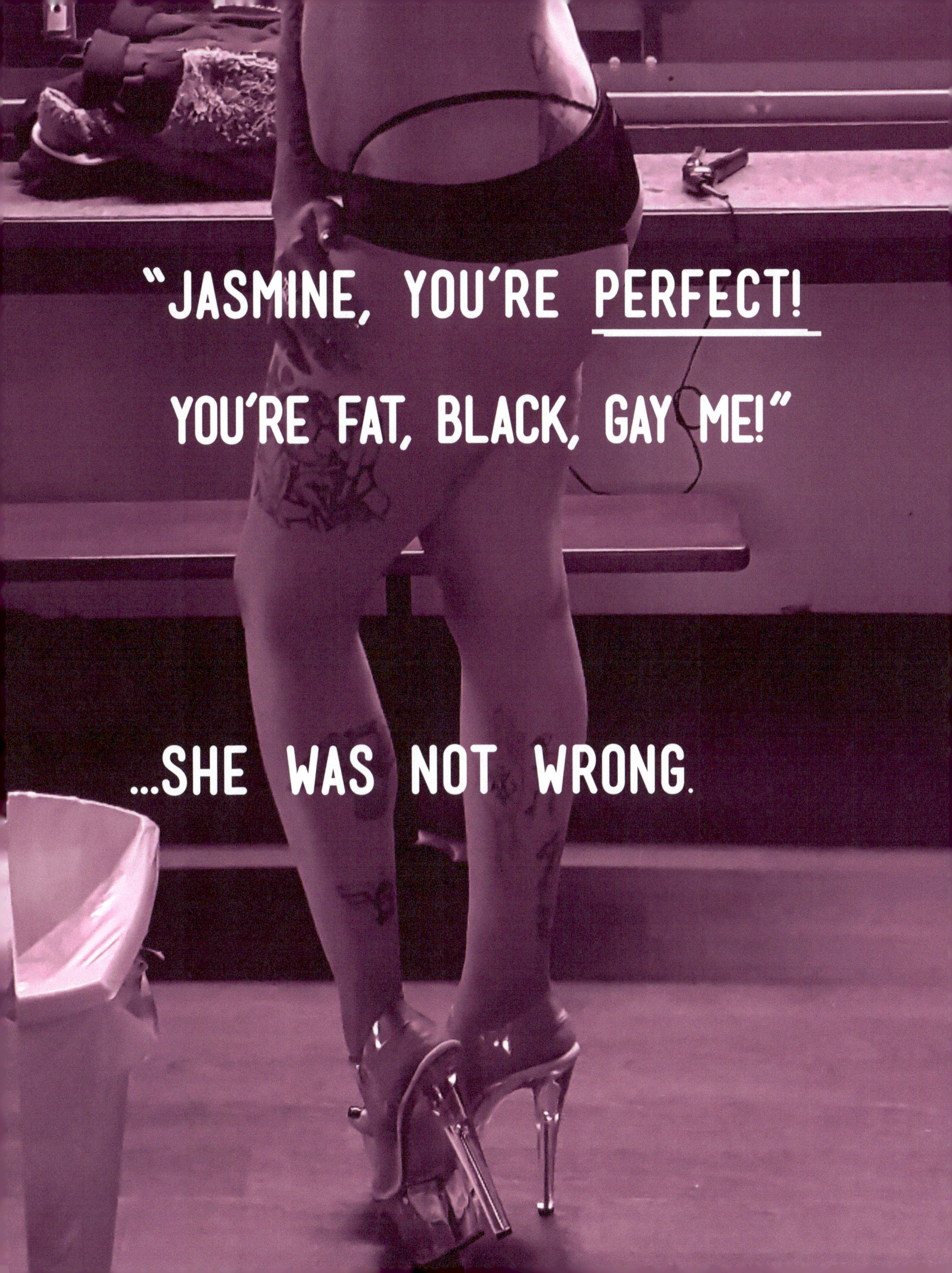
"JASMINE, YOU'RE PERFECT!
YOU'RE FAT, BLACK, GAY ME!"
...SHE WAS NOT WRONG.

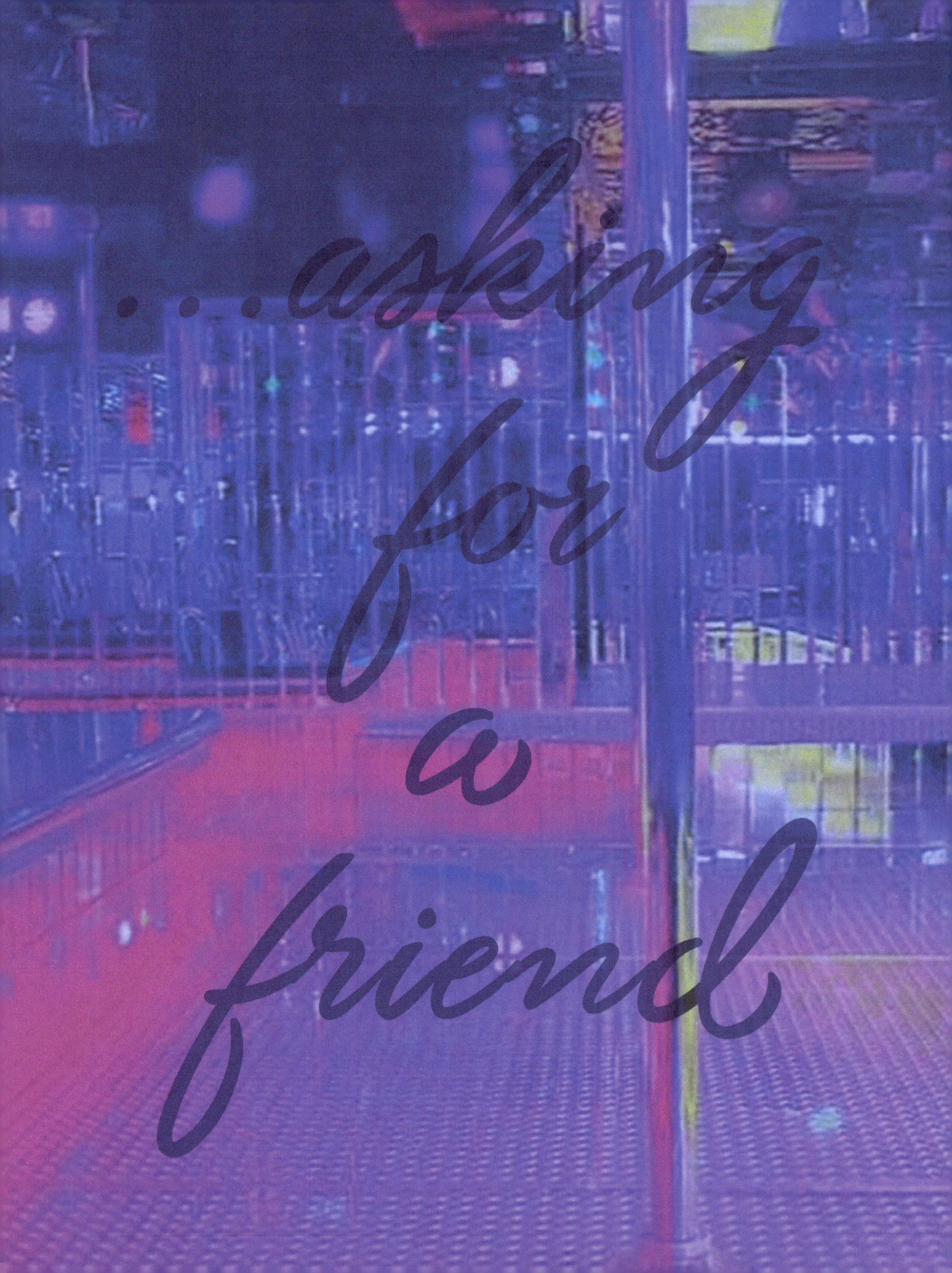

...asking
for
a
friend

YOU EVER LOSE THE ABILITY TO SEE
YOURSELF…

LIKE, NOT BELIEVING THAT ITS YOU
IN THE MIRROR, MAGNIFYING ALL
YOUR UGLINESS, AND MALICIOUSLY
TAKING VALIDATION FROM ANY SOURCE…

TO THE POINT THAT YOU CANNOT SUSTAIN
REAL RELATIONSHIPS OUTSIDE THIS
PLACE?

YA, ME NEITHER, I WAS ASKING
FOR A FRIEND.

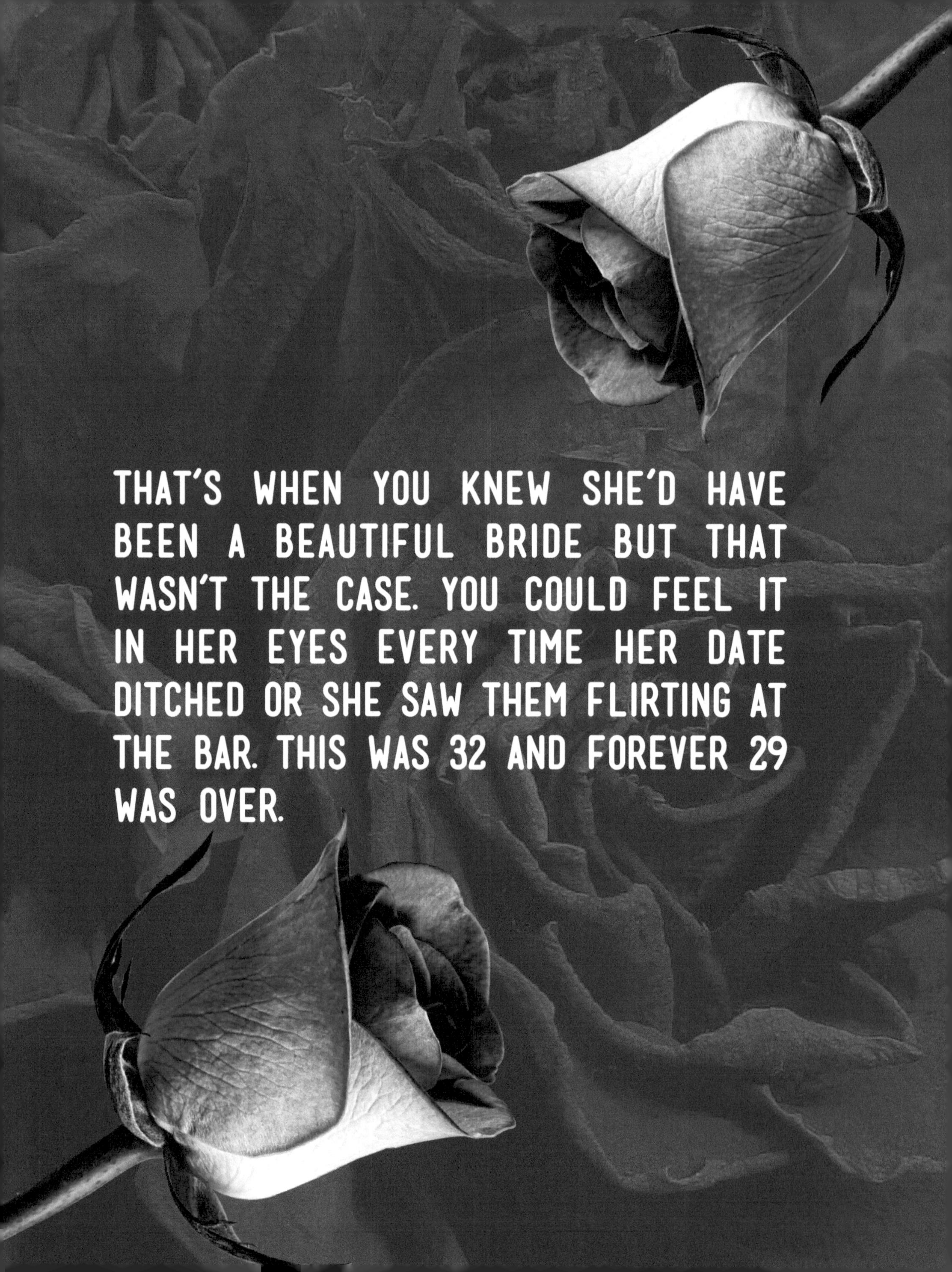
THAT'S WHEN YOU KNEW SHE'D HAVE BEEN A BEAUTIFUL BRIDE BUT THAT WASN'T THE CASE. YOU COULD FEEL IT IN HER EYES EVERY TIME HER DATE DITCHED OR SHE SAW THEM FLIRTING AT THE BAR. THIS WAS 32 AND FOREVER 29 WAS OVER.

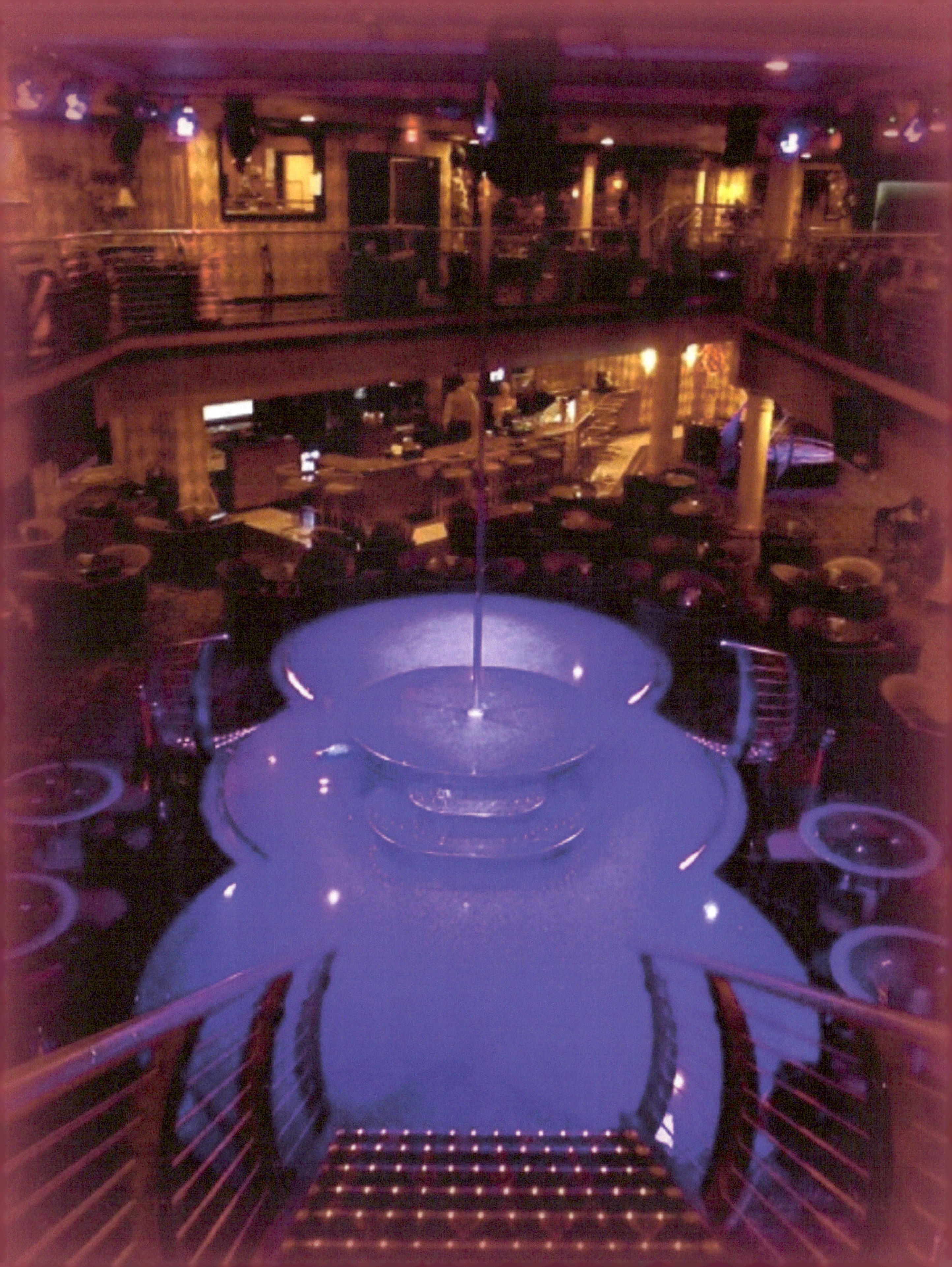

"DID YOU HEAR THAT THE YOUNG GIRLS ARE STARTING TO CALL CARDI B AND BLAC CHYNA THE SAINTS OF STRIPPING?"

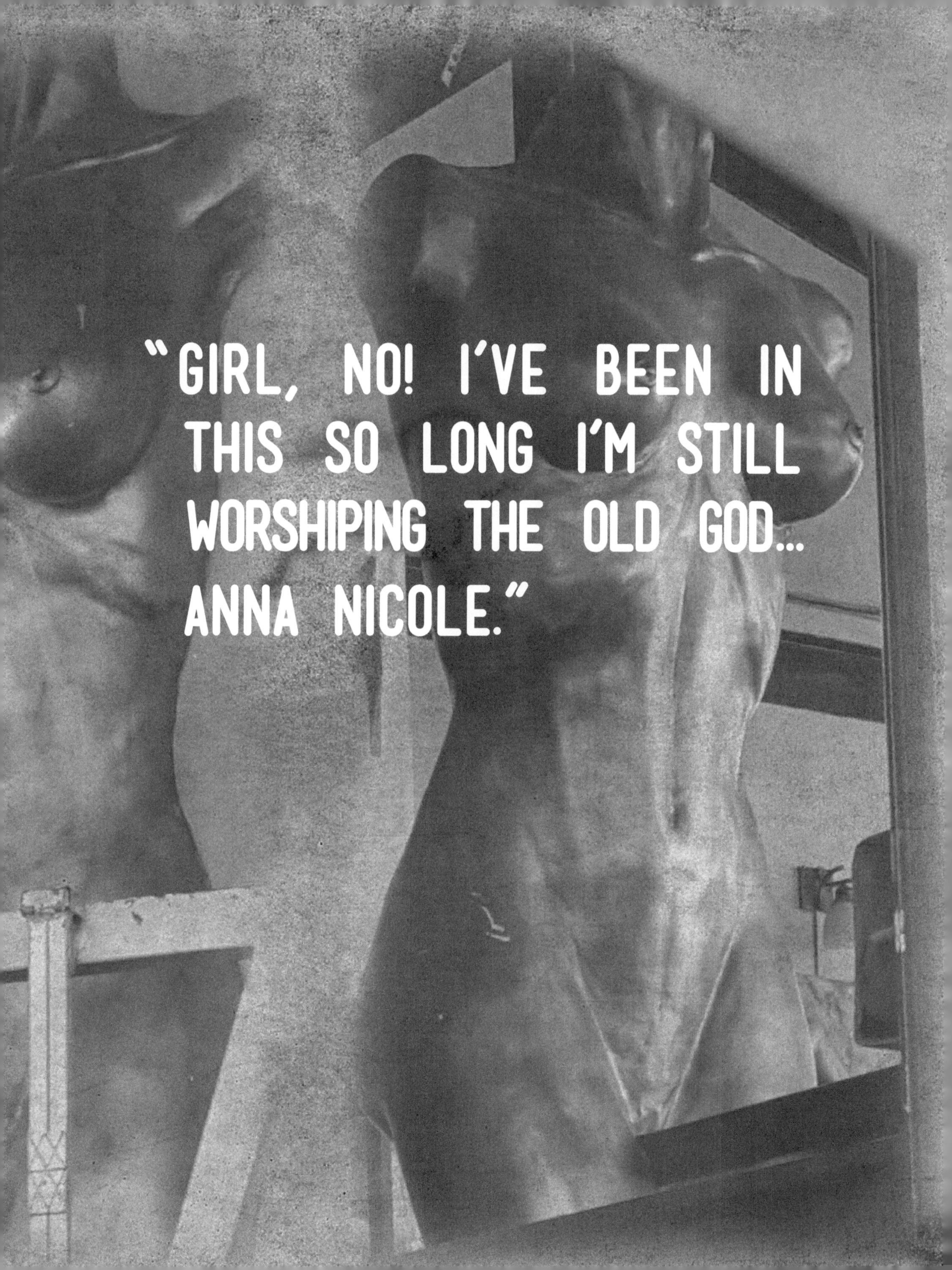

"GIRL, NO! I'VE BEEN IN THIS SO LONG I'M STILL WORSHIPING THE OLD GOD... ANNA NICOLE."

On Clubs

There once was a rat—
we named him Ralph;
he lived in the second
floor dressingroom
bathroom.

He fell through
the floor one slow
Tuesday evening on
a dancer named
Goddess.

"Who was that?"

"Little Nikki, because big Nikki was Raina here. But Raina is actually Nikki and Janessa is Jessica, but her sis, Layla, is here, too, and she's Helena now."

After 6 more shots just decides to call everyone 'Hun' or 'Baby.'

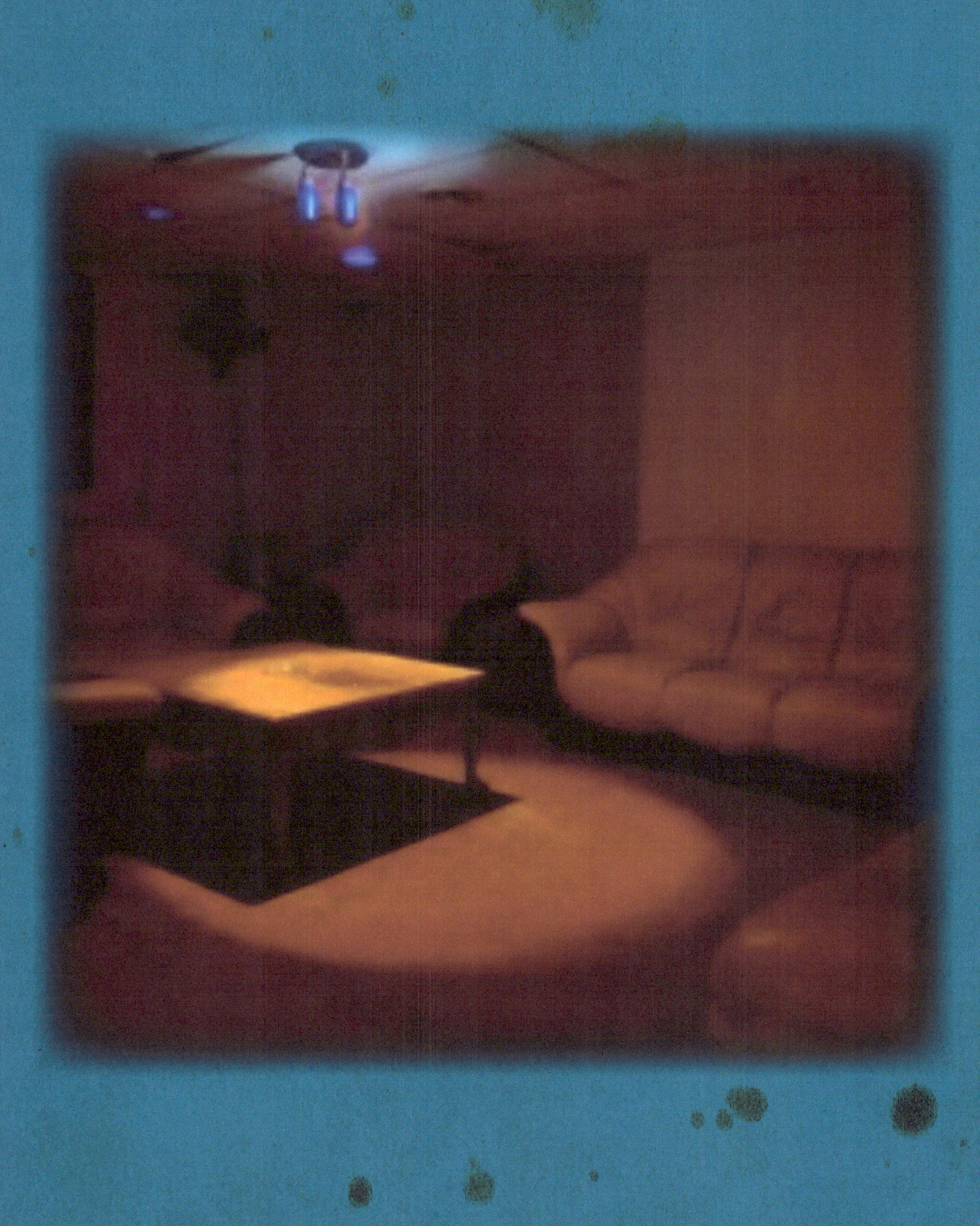

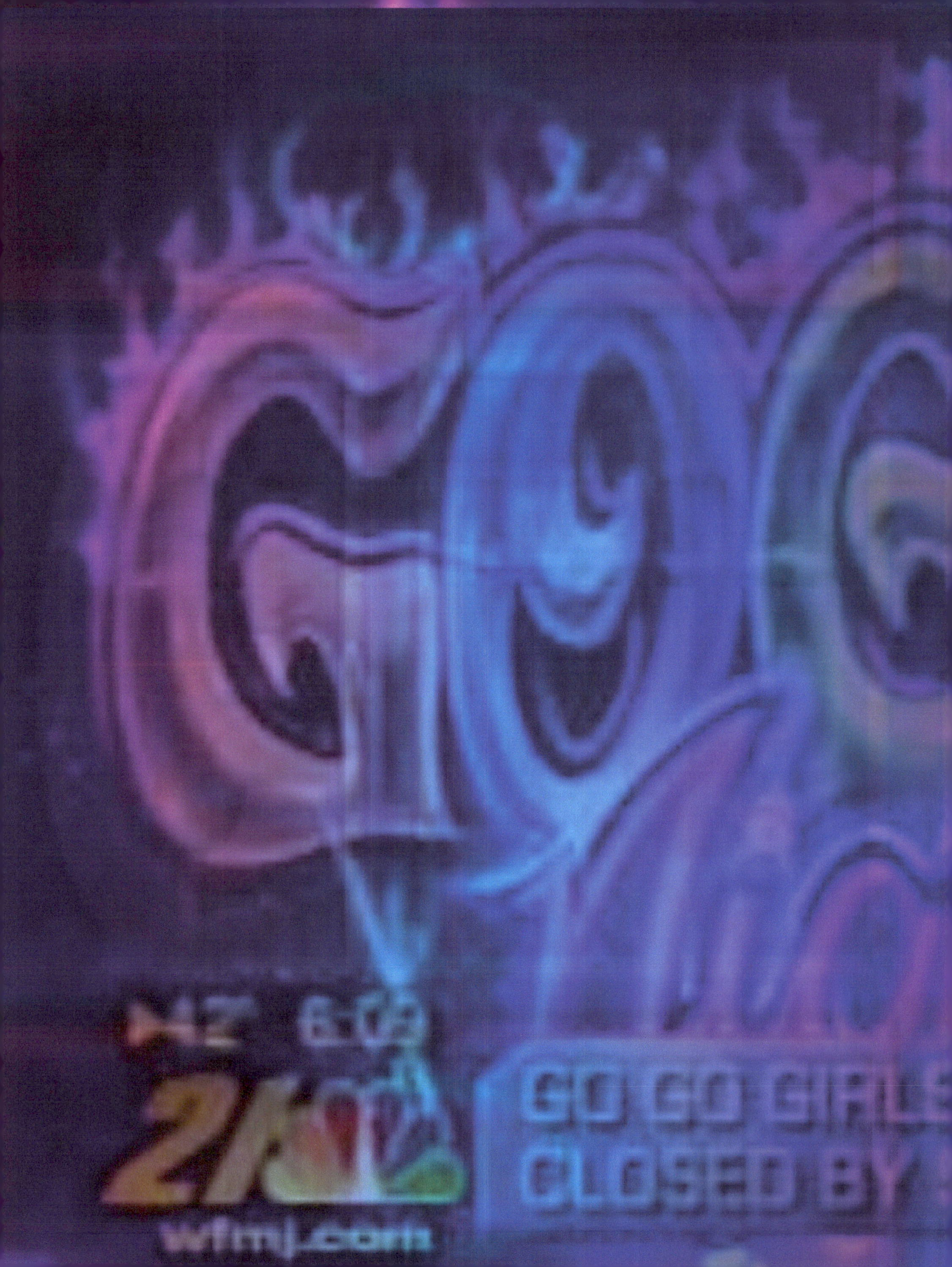
GO GO GIRLS
CLOSED BY
wftl.com

The manager was named Rick, but we called him the Crypt Keeper because, let's face it, he was old and looked like the character from that TV show.

Every night he would remind everyone, "If you need the cameras off let me know beforehand and I'll turn them off."

Well, he never came back. Not because of any trouble— I heard he got sick. There was a funeral a short time after.

"Who the...?

What the fuck?!

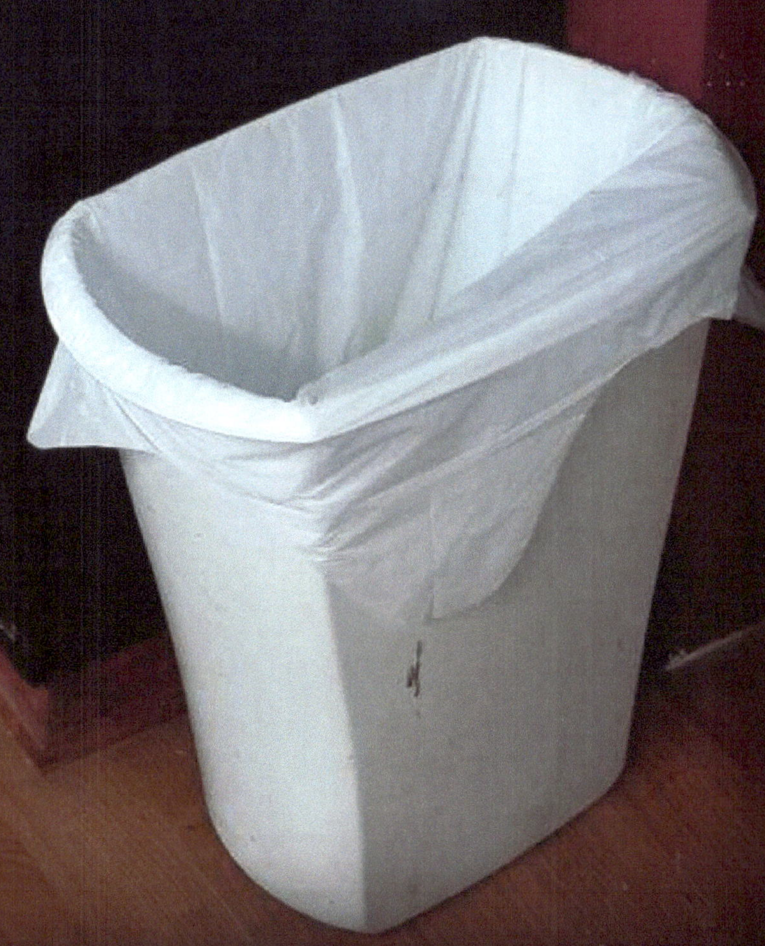
LAYLA PISSED IN THE TRASH CAN *AGAIN?!"*

—an ode
to every club's
slipper talk—

"Wait, I was in the bathroom...
I missed it! Is she calling us
whores when she just got fired
for offering to suck a customer's
dick for money?"

"<u>YEP!</u>" All the girls hiding in the
back answer in unison.

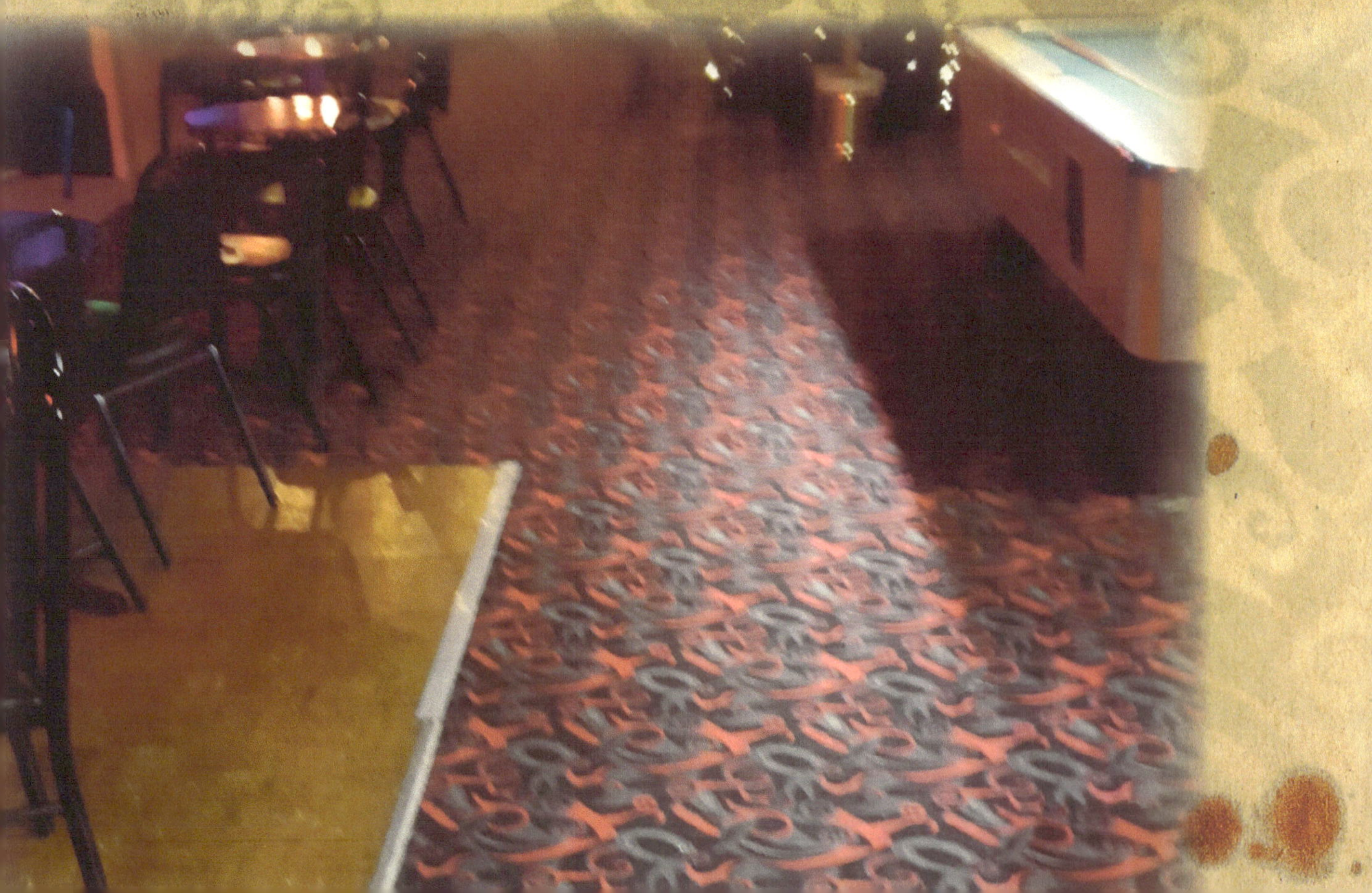

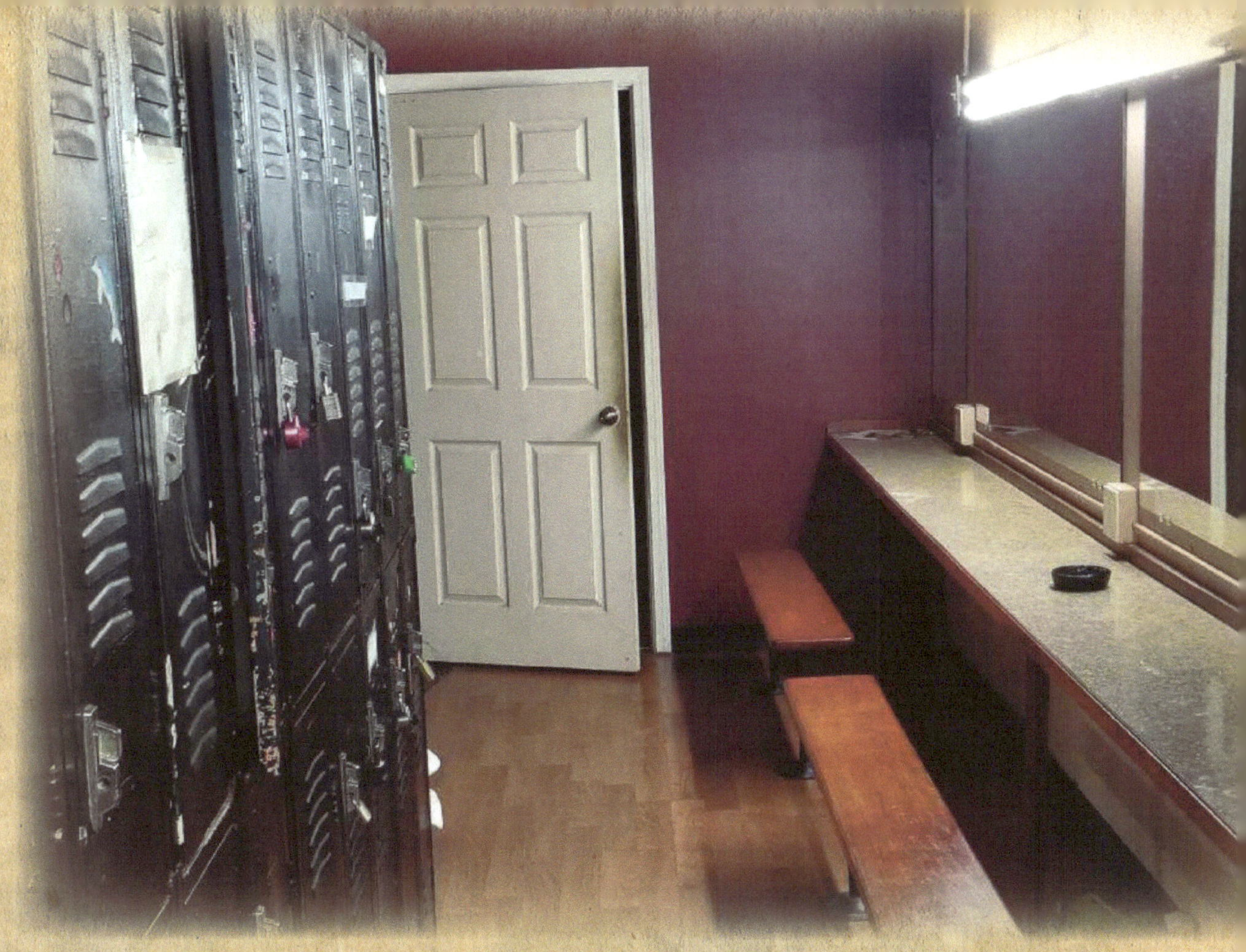

And in the following silence we can all hear the bouncers' keys jangling as they wrangle her out the back door all the way to her ride.

"Someone had to explain, "'Bands Will Make Her Dance' to me," Ruby exclaimed.

"Okay—what they tell you?" I replied exhausted. She was nearly 50 and a white lady who used to date politicians and do porn.

"It's the garters because it holds their asses up when they are too big and muscley to move on their own!" Fuck she was so happy with her reply.

I respond, "That song is about money. Like the paper that holds a bank stack together."

Ruby refused to accept this.

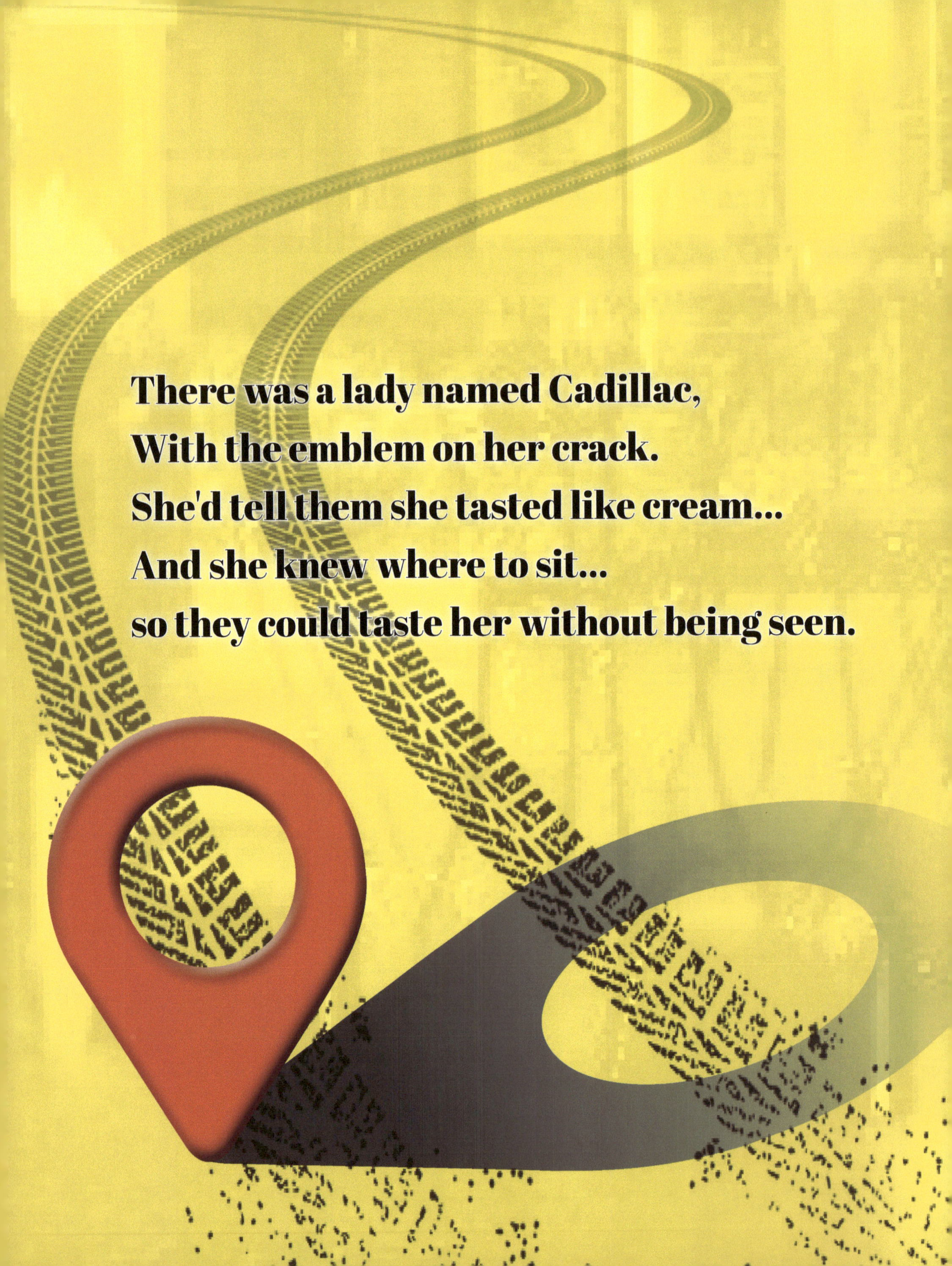

There was a lady named Cadillac,
With the emblem on her crack.
She'd tell them she tasted like cream...
And she knew where to sit...
so they could taste her without being seen.

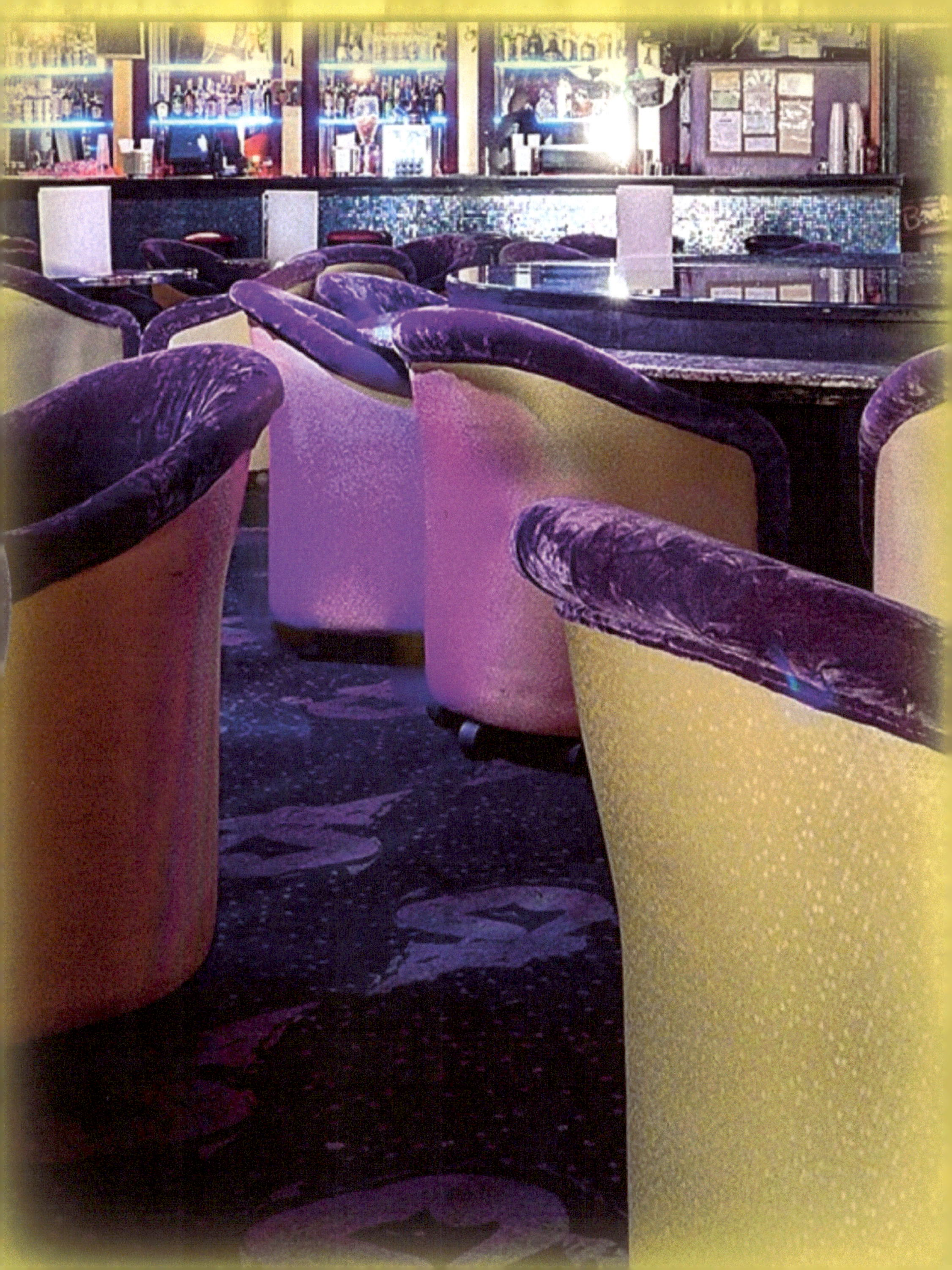

a current reflection:

Sandy an old manager from another club shows up on my shift to sell outfits. She comes in with another dancer, stays the whole shift and leaves by cane and aid. She was in her early 70's with custody of her grandkids, we would all buy something time and again. An old hustler, she'd make your customer buy the outfit for you any chance she got. I haven't seen or heard of her in more than 5 years.

Little Bop Girl*—A southern white girl who is falling over, running around the club singing Cardi B.

She climbs upstairs drunk yelling, "If I hear one more white guy 'I don't dance now I make money moves' while singing the song, I'm gonna lynch'em."

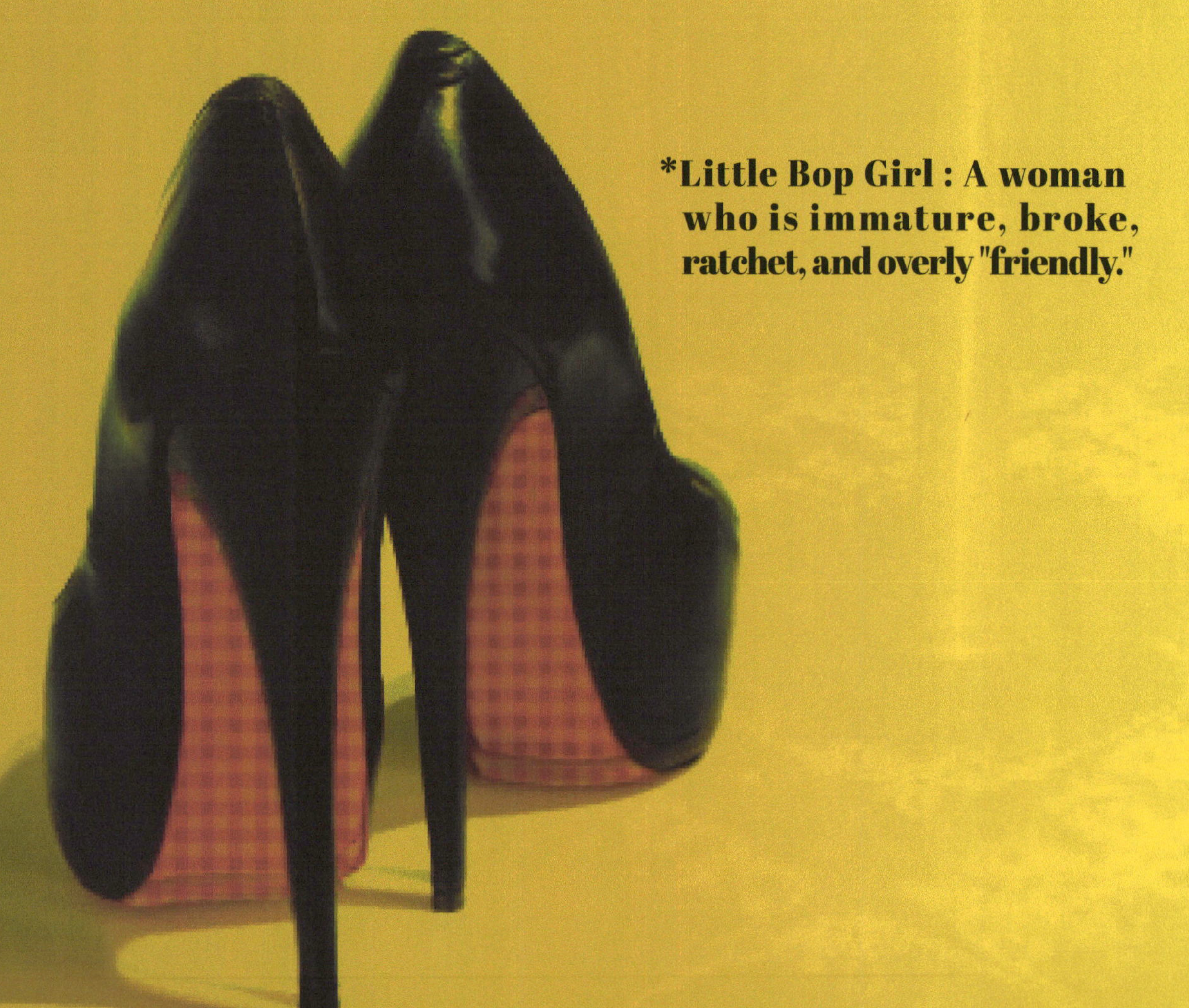

***Little Bop Girl : A woman who is immature, broke, ratchet, and overly "friendly."**

Every black girl in the dressing room responds with a long hard pause.

...“Can I say that? I can say that, can’t I?”

TIM BURTON TYPE VOICEOVER:

—

But no. No, she could not say that. And they never trusted or spoke with the girl again.

—

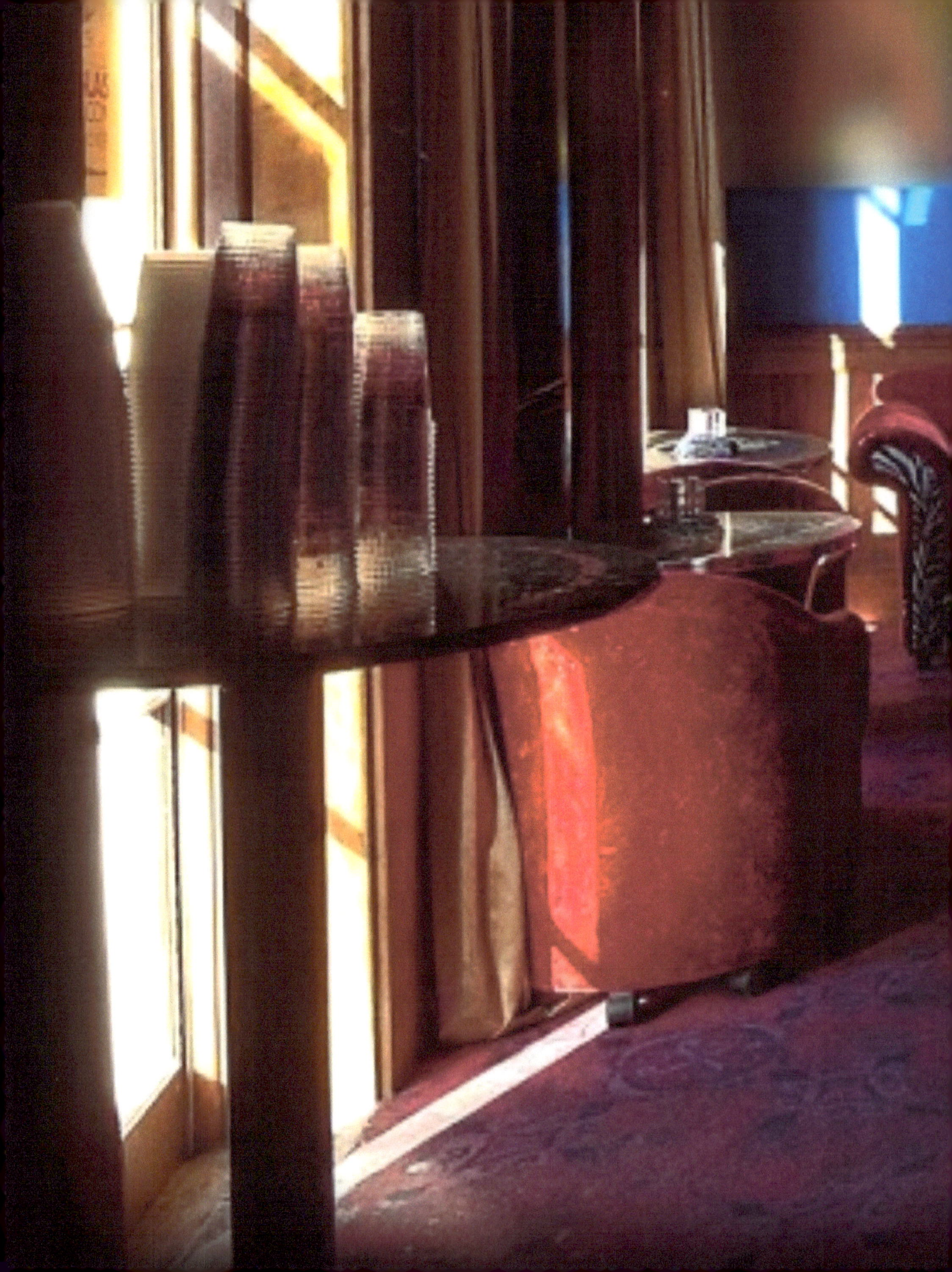

"You ever see someone puke in a champagne bucket, beat up their husband, run barefoot down Bourbon street, then come back to the *clurrrbbb* to see if they had time left on the room?"

Von Satan sideeyes me from the VIP bar as my nightmare couple stumbles back up the stairs.

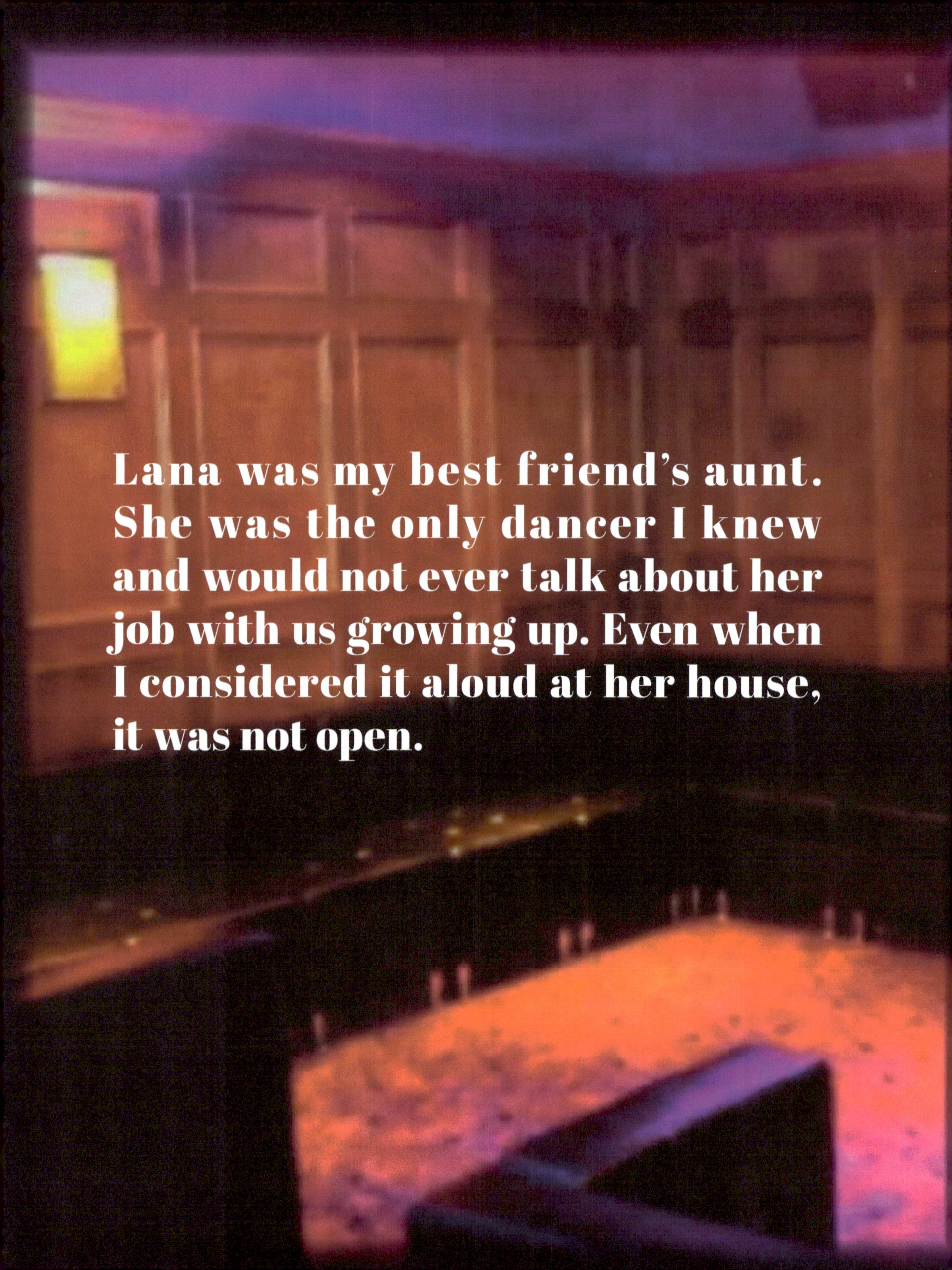

Lana was my best friend's aunt. She was the only dancer I knew and would not ever talk about her job with us growing up. Even when I considered it aloud at her house, it was not open.

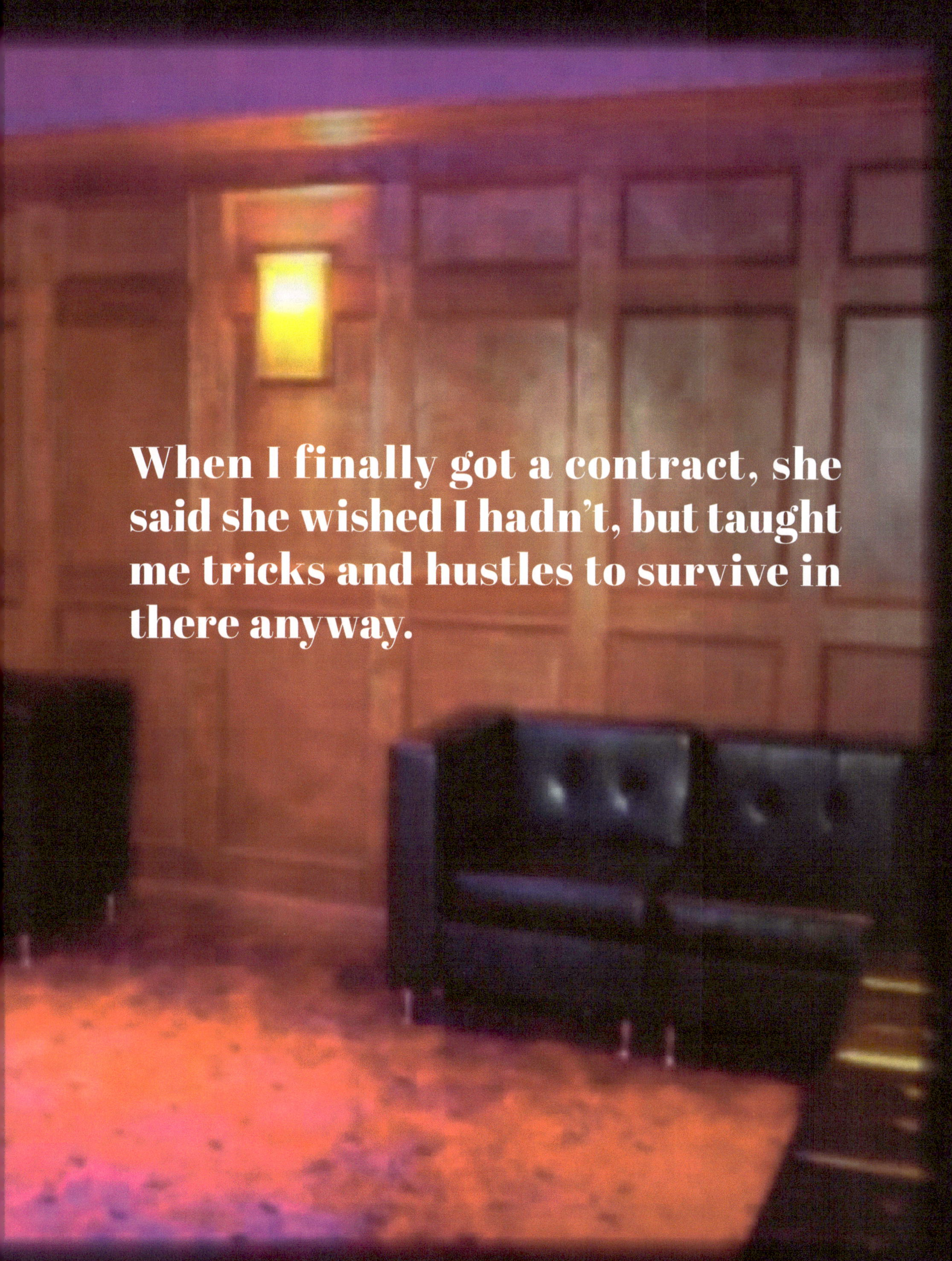
When I finally got a contract, she said she wished I hadn't, but taught me tricks and hustles to survive in there anyway.

On Family Matters

Out of all the disturbing things we see and hear, there's none so strong as hearing someone called to the stage whose stage name is your actual daughter's name while wasted at some god awful hour of the night.

i got pregnant by him
on that couch.

bitch, that's nasty, i know
his wife!

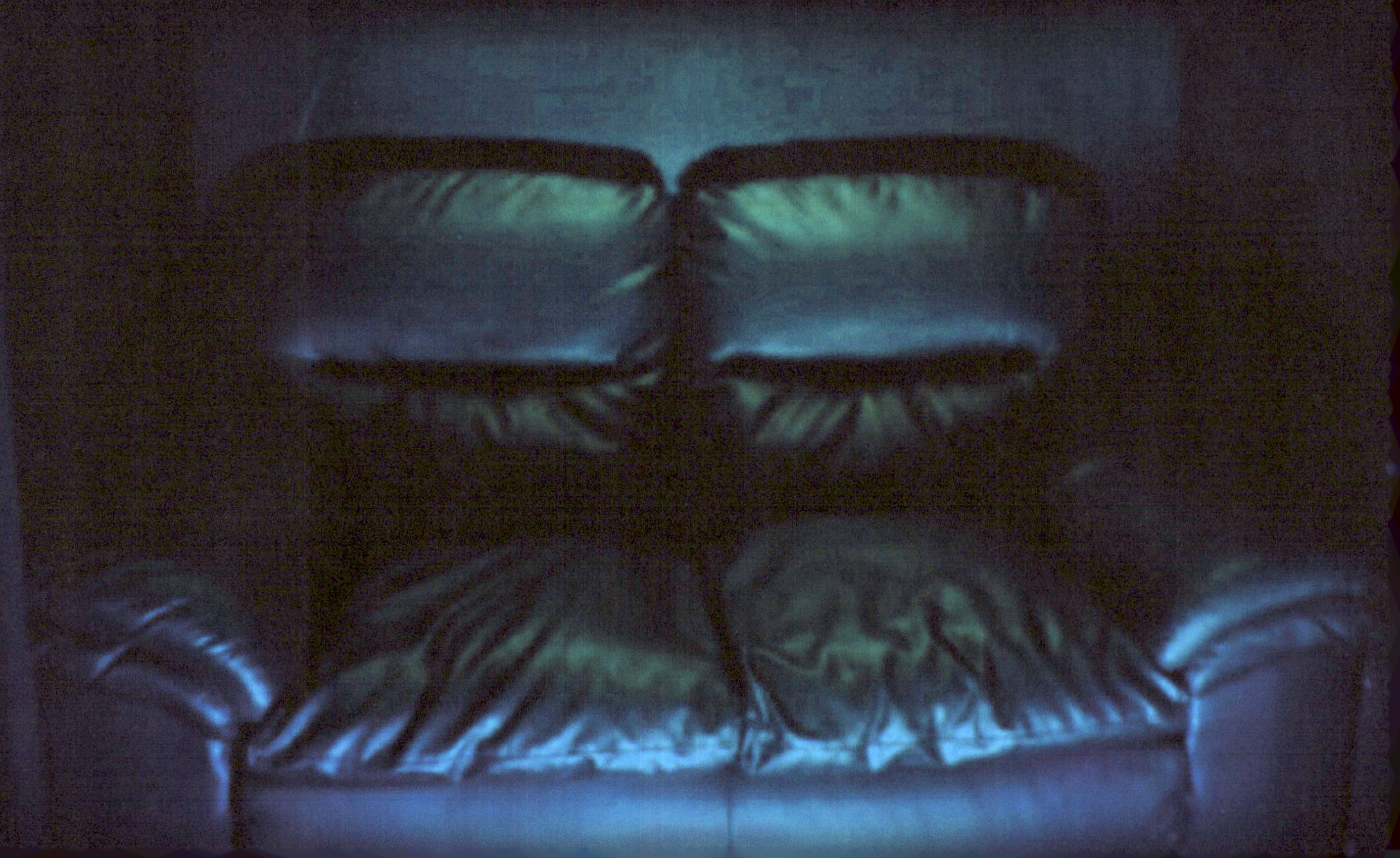

i know her, too.

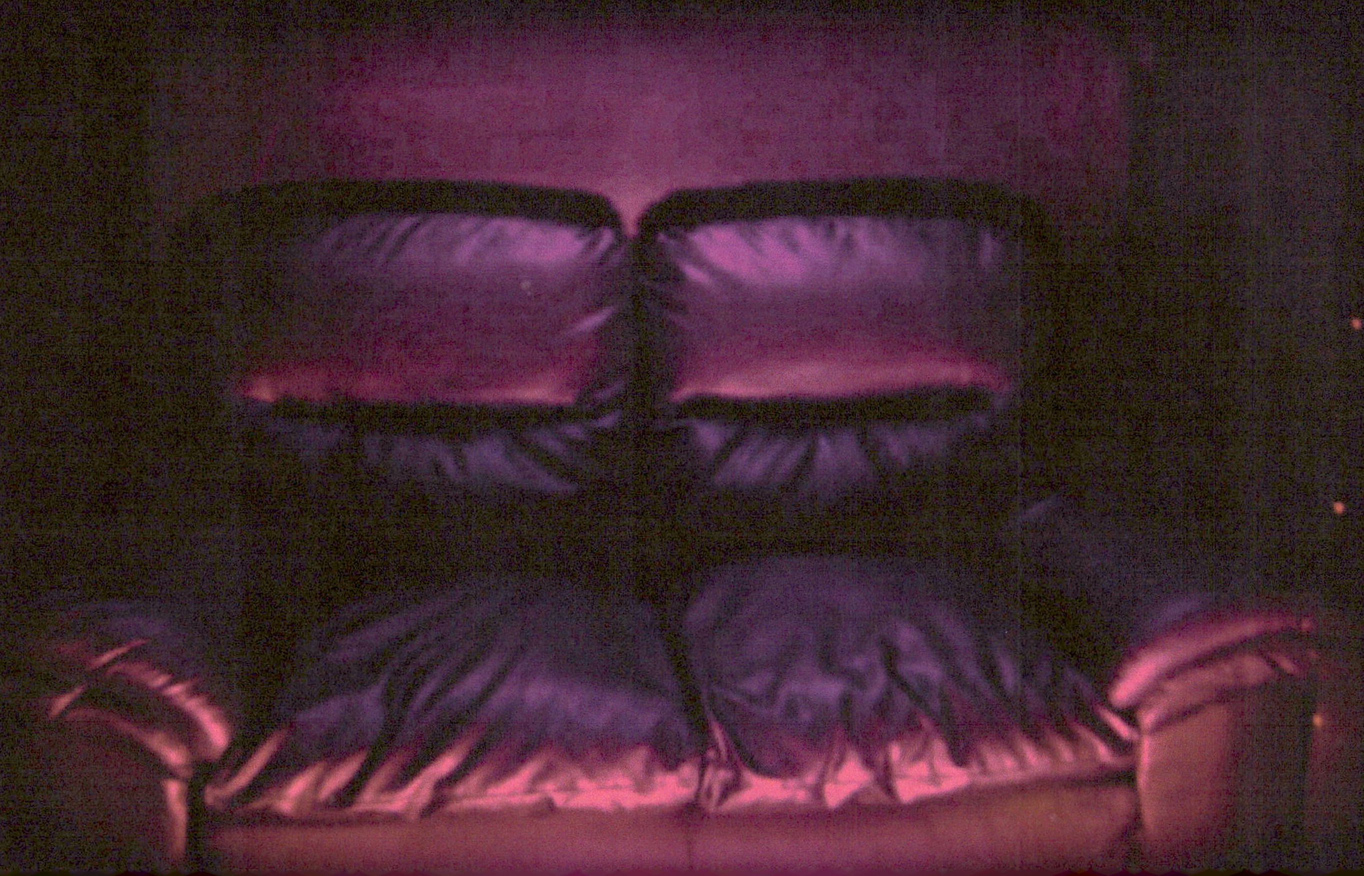

Strangest thing ever received in a garter belt was a wedding invitation printed on computer paper and folded around some ones.

Most of the girls got one; the few who did not, were mad.

The couple was older, like retired, the man, a biker. They came in a lot, like every weekend for a year.

None of us went to the wedding and they never came back.

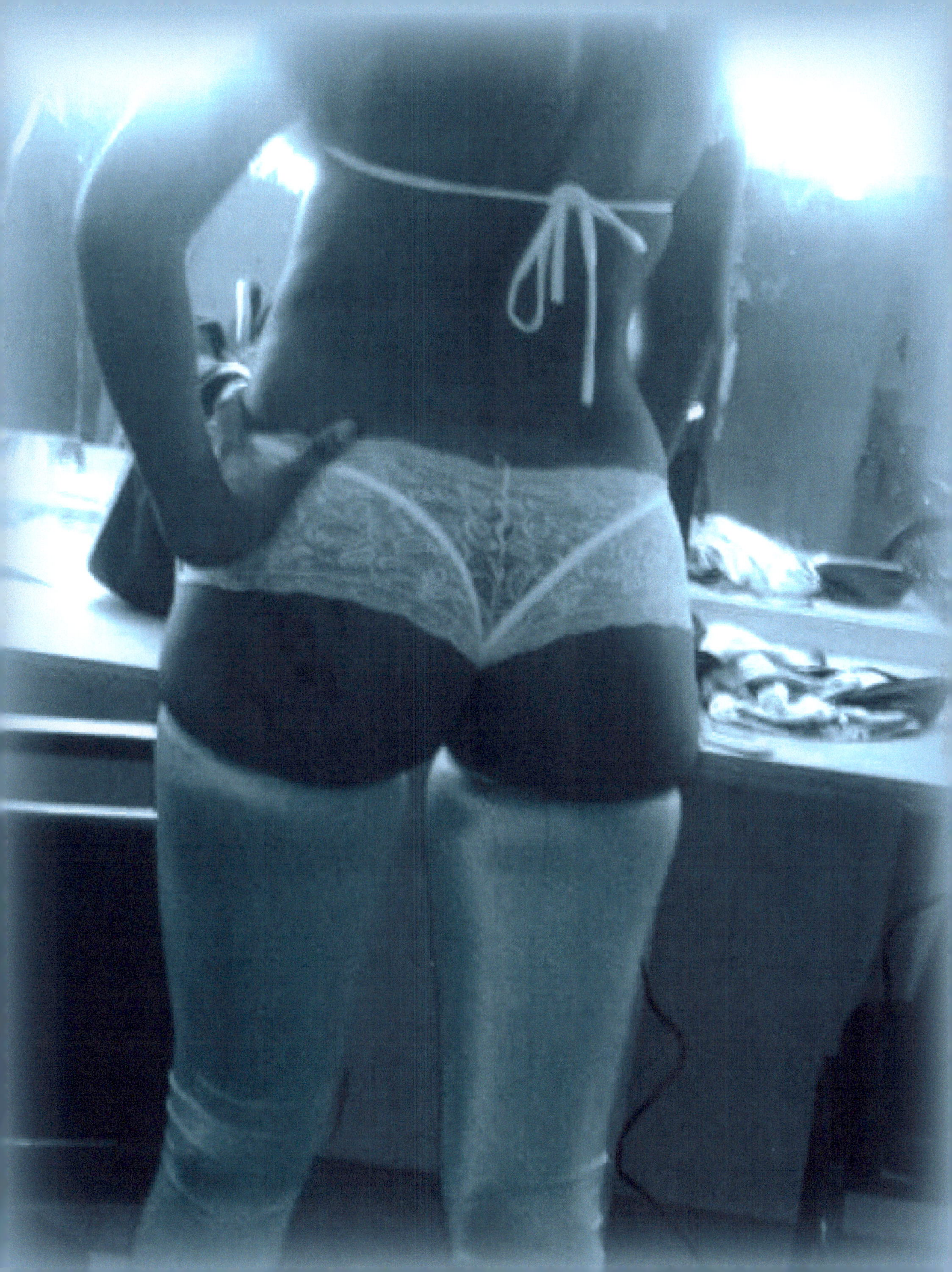

"All I know is if I saw any of her customers at my daughter's school, I'd have a mother fucking problem."

Brianna was 4'9" and had the body of a 6th grader. She was 18 and had a creepy old man and ghetto boy following.

●—●

A tribute to the skeeze of strip club pedophiles who act out scouting and raspberry fantasies in these spaces because the girls here are 18 whether they look it or not?

A crippling disturbing public service?

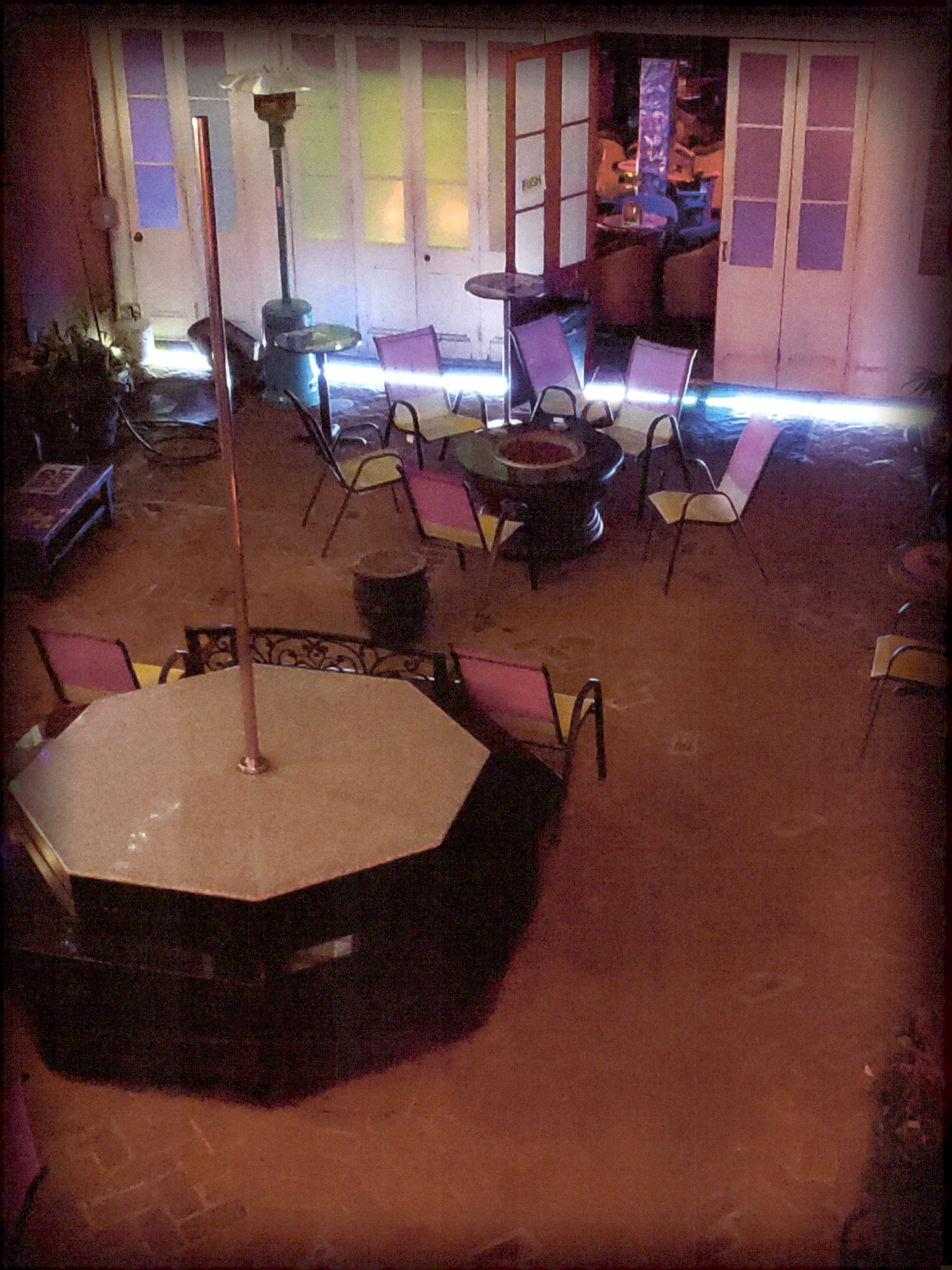
PUSH

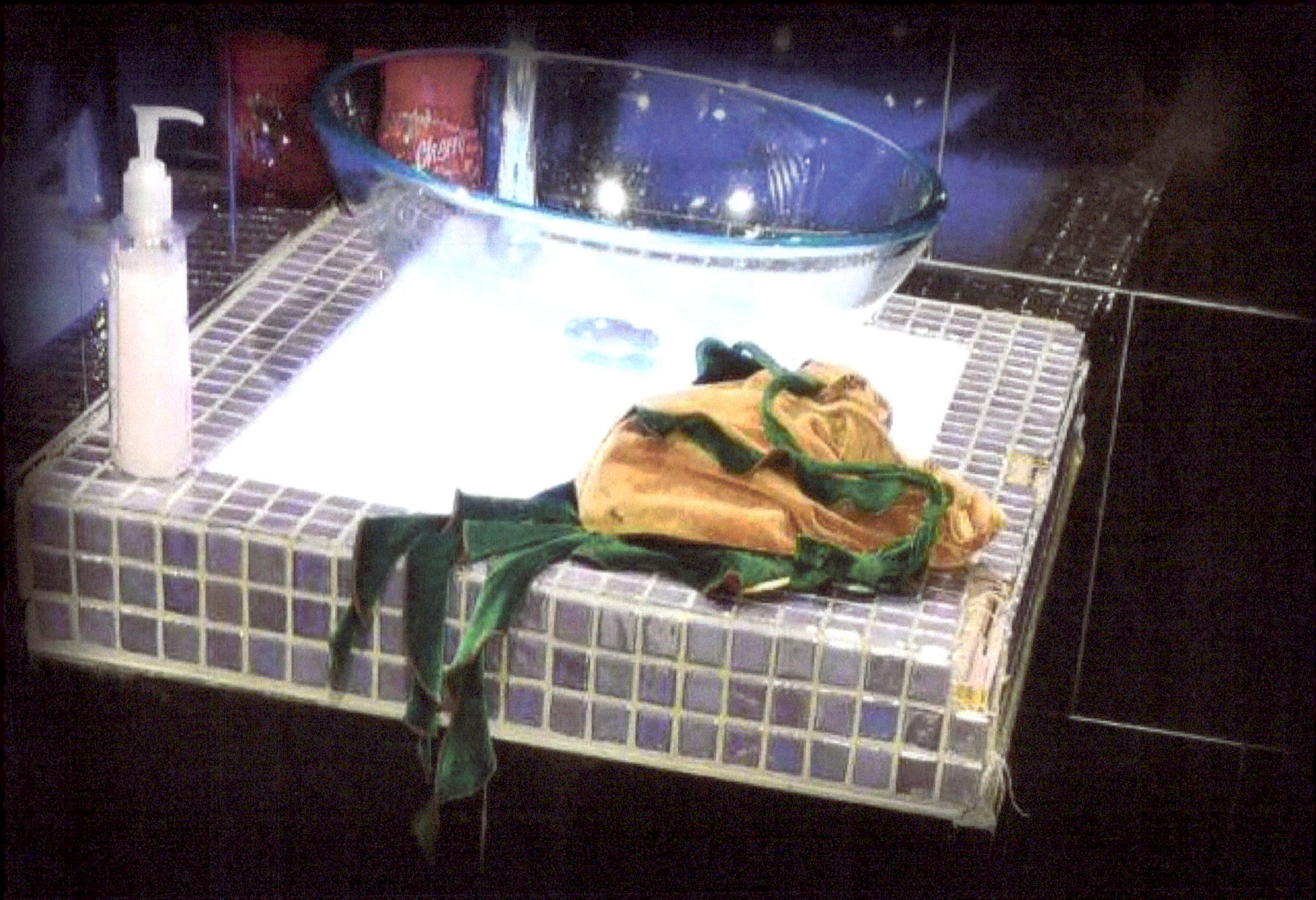

Dancer Name	Number of Dances	Dancer Paid
Danny	|||| ||| |||| ||||||	
Sazzu	||	||
Abby		|||	
Caliente	|||| ||||	
Cloe		|||	
Bella	|||| |||| ||	|||| |||| ||
Samantha	|||| ||||		|||| ||||	
Gomez	—	—
Kat	|||| |||	
Scarlet	|||| ||	||||	
Tyler		
Karlis				

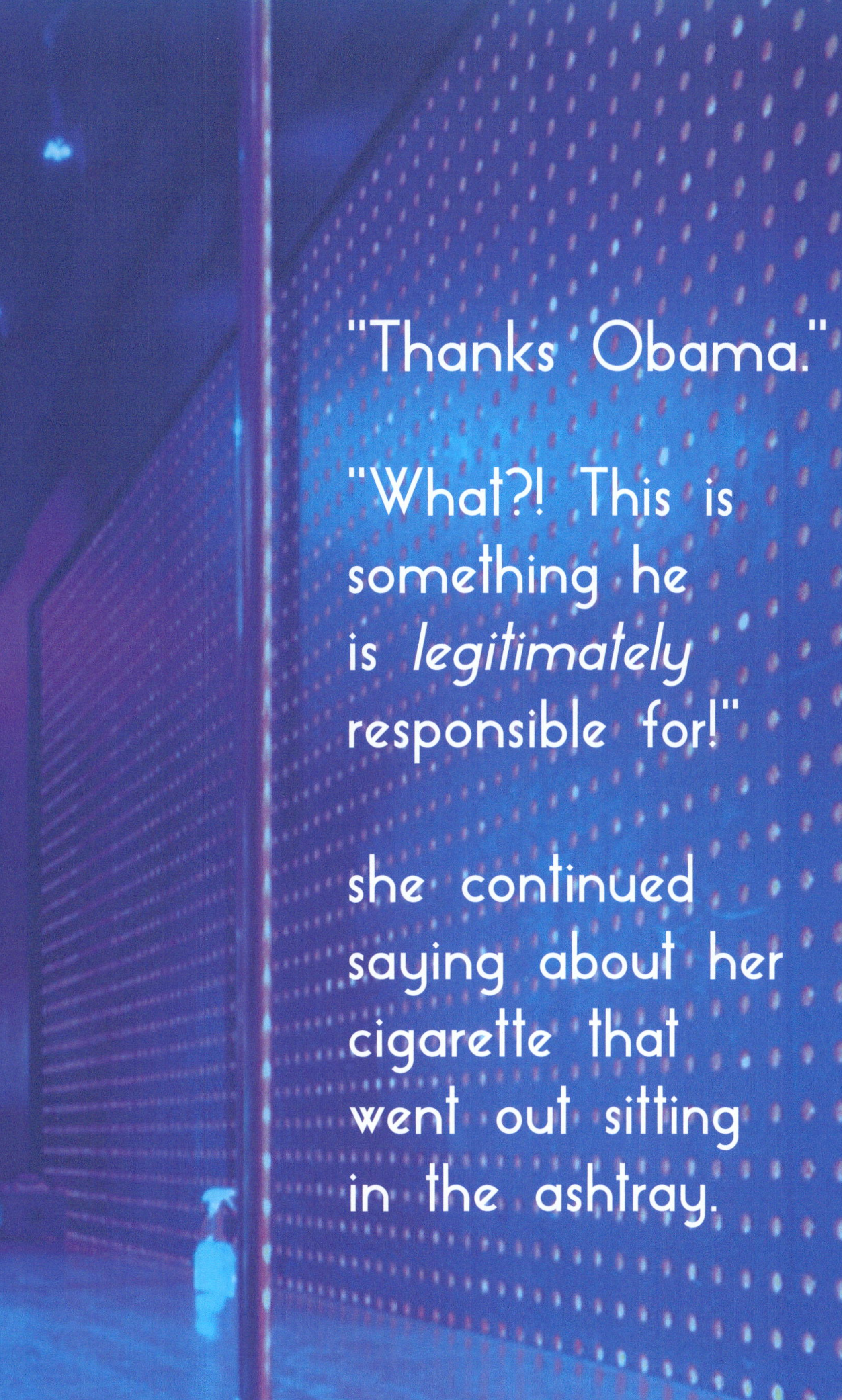
"Thanks Obama."

"What?! This is something he is *legitimately* responsible for!"

she continued saying about her cigarette that went out sitting in the ashtray.

There are two types
of manager:

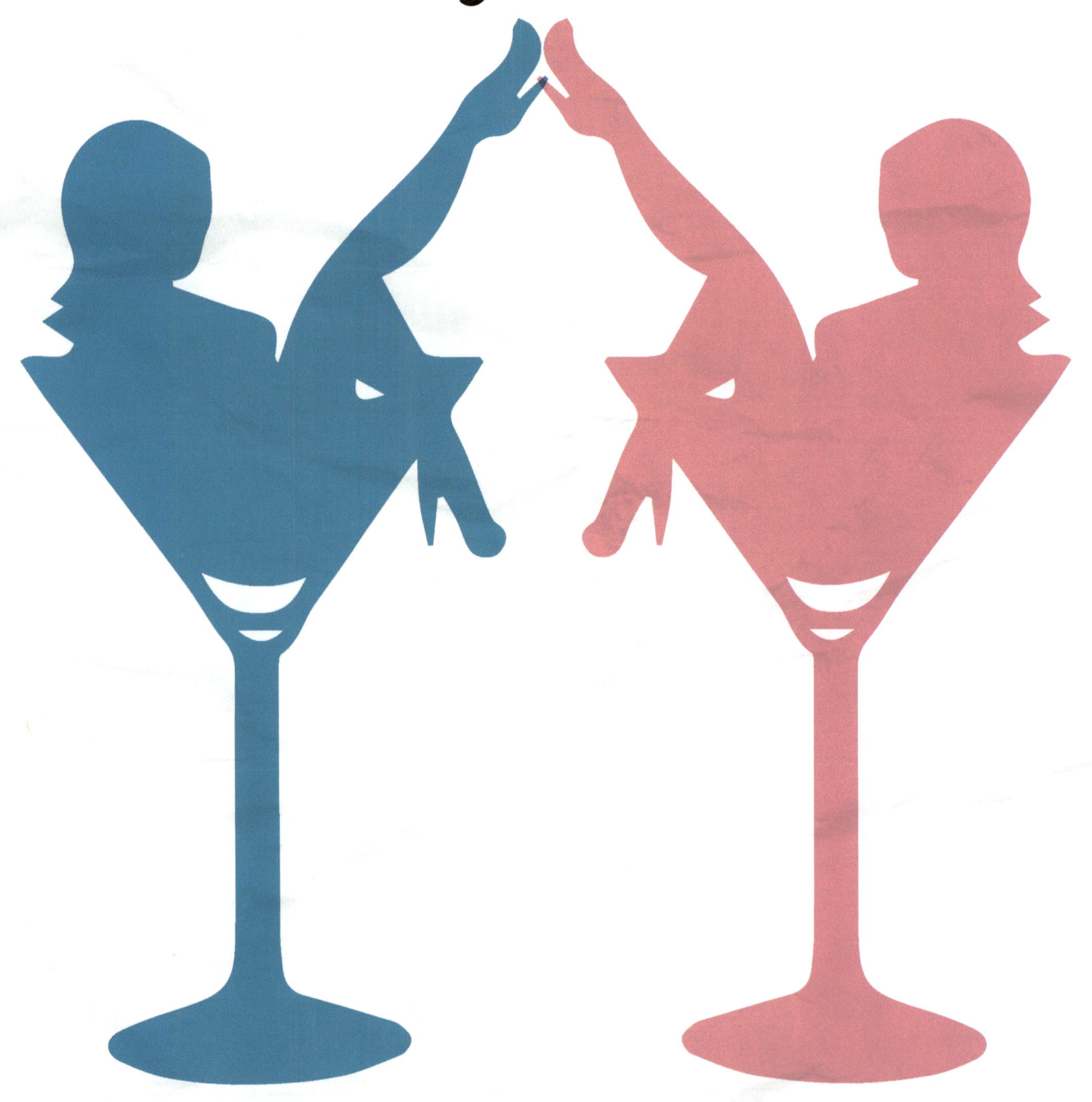

"He is going to
make someone so
happy one day"

and

"How the fuck
does he have a
real girlfriend?"

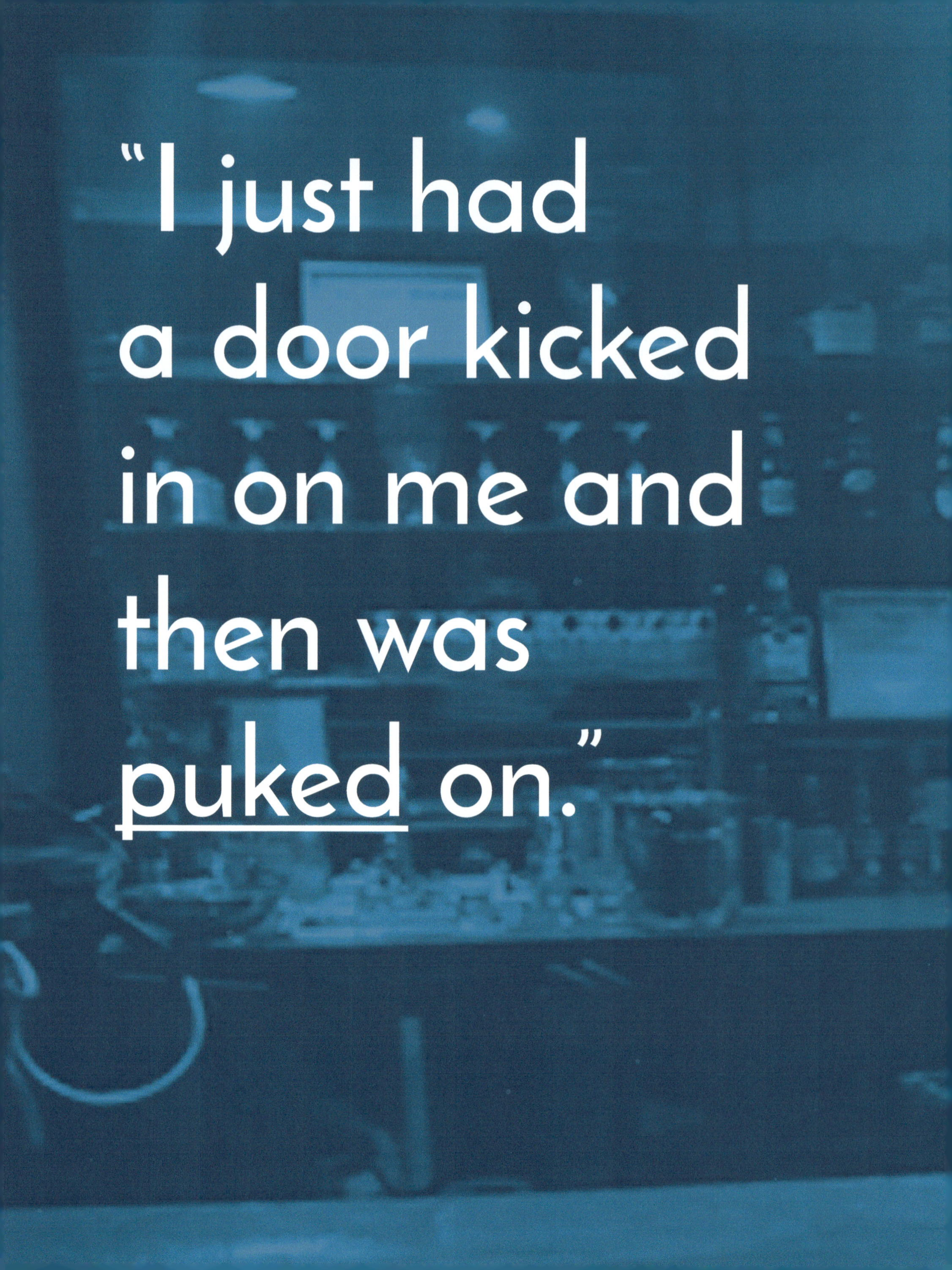

"I just had
a door kicked
in on me and
then was
<u>puked</u> on."

Explaining simultaneously why:

(1) she deserved two shots despite the "one drink per hour" policy

and why

(2) she stole a customer's Halloween costume.

Danny, once while overseas dancing on contract, saw one dancer beat another girl's face in with an ashtray over stolen yogurt. It happened in their arranged housing after a shift some night. They were told to leave her dead in the living space and go to bed. The dead girl was gone by the time they woke up.

When I recently talked to her about this, she corrected me: "The yogurt thing was a stabbing ftr."

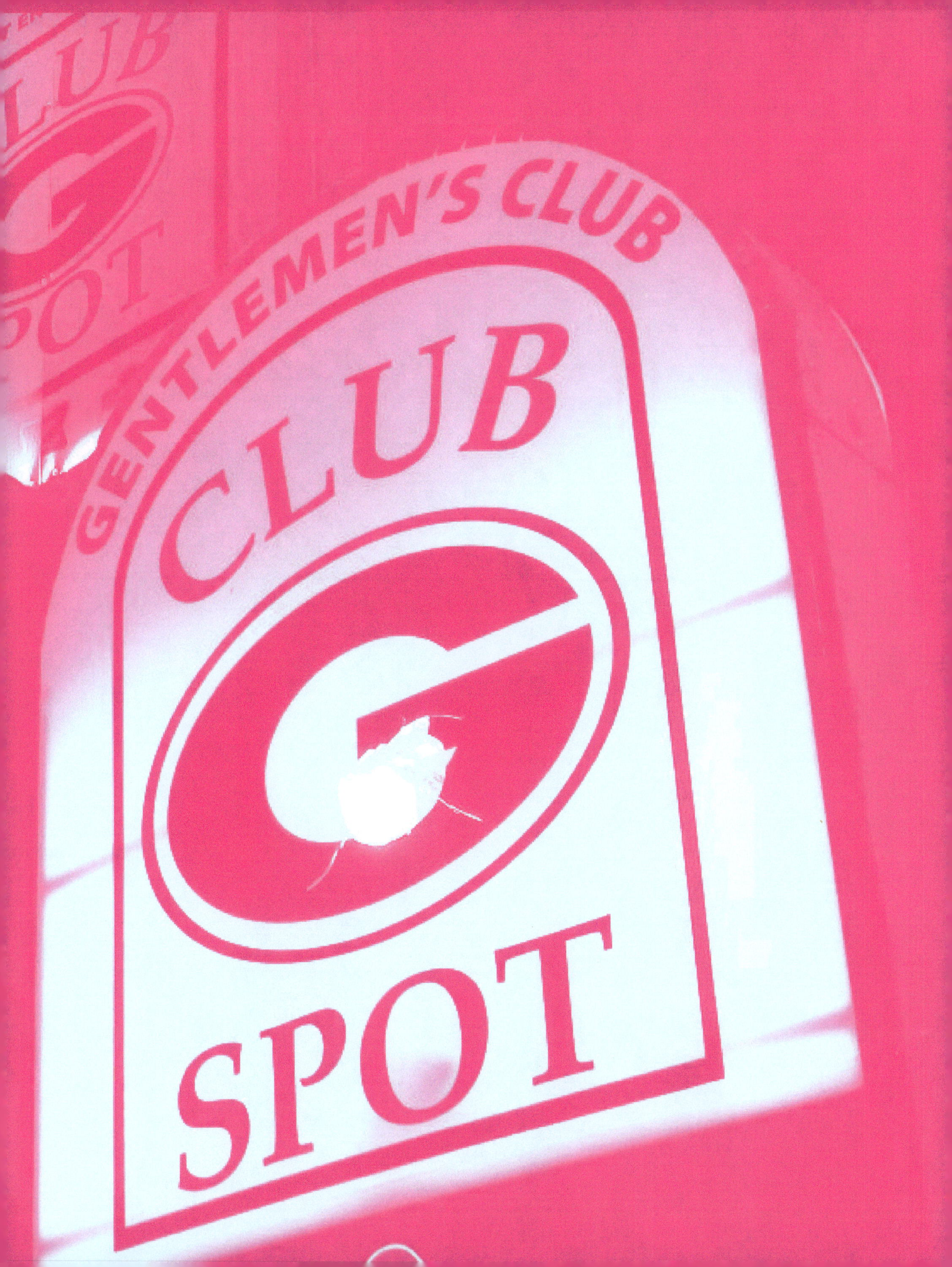

GENTLEMEN'S CLUB
CLUB
G
SPOT

On Survival and Scams

SCAM STORYTIME:

I knew a girl who gave the best lap dances. All she did was sit and grind. I asked her once why she did that, thinking about how nasty men's crotches just are. She then detailed the way she worked her knees about a man's pocket and coerced it out of the pocket into the couch. She would then take a super long time to redress and after the man left empty the cash and shove the wallet back into the couch. This is my new favorite way to give dances.

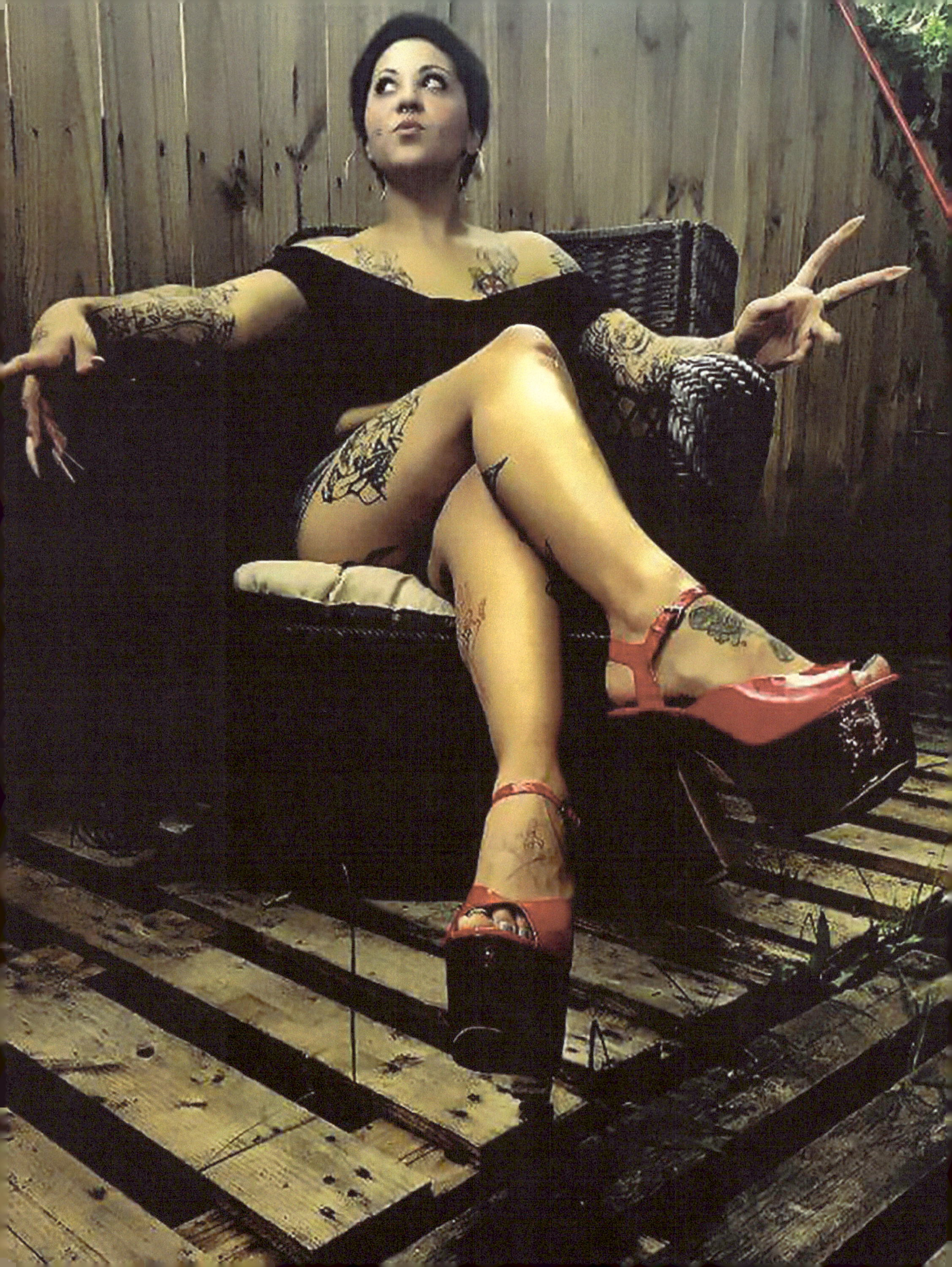

I came around the corner, standing 6'3"
in my heels to a very small baby stripper
screaming at a friend of mine. Without
thinking, I lifted her off her feet by the
neck just to pause the noise.

Management came and apologized to ME.
They surpassed the crying barely legal
babe and apologized to the irritated
veteran dancer.

That's management for ya.

#thearistocrats

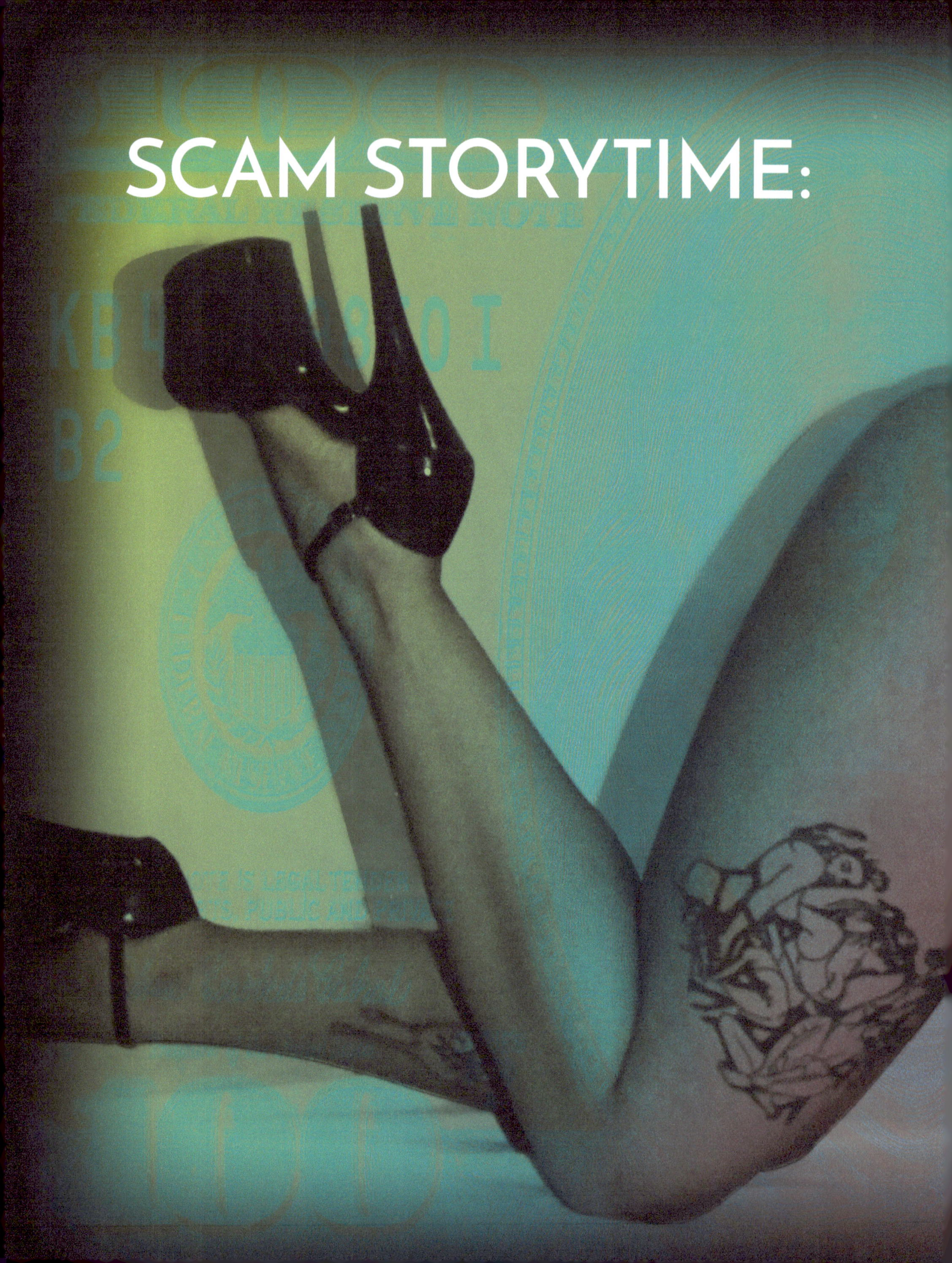
SCAM STORYTIME:

Victoria and whoever would run the ATM. A girl would bring a gentleman over to use the machine. She'd wait until money was dispensed, do a split standing up. The unsuspecting man would distract himself and another dancer would swipe the cash and hit cancel in the machine. We'd all giggle and tell him it timed out. Vikki took 50 percent and everyone else split the till. She hated being called Vikki. She lived in hotel efficiency apartments.

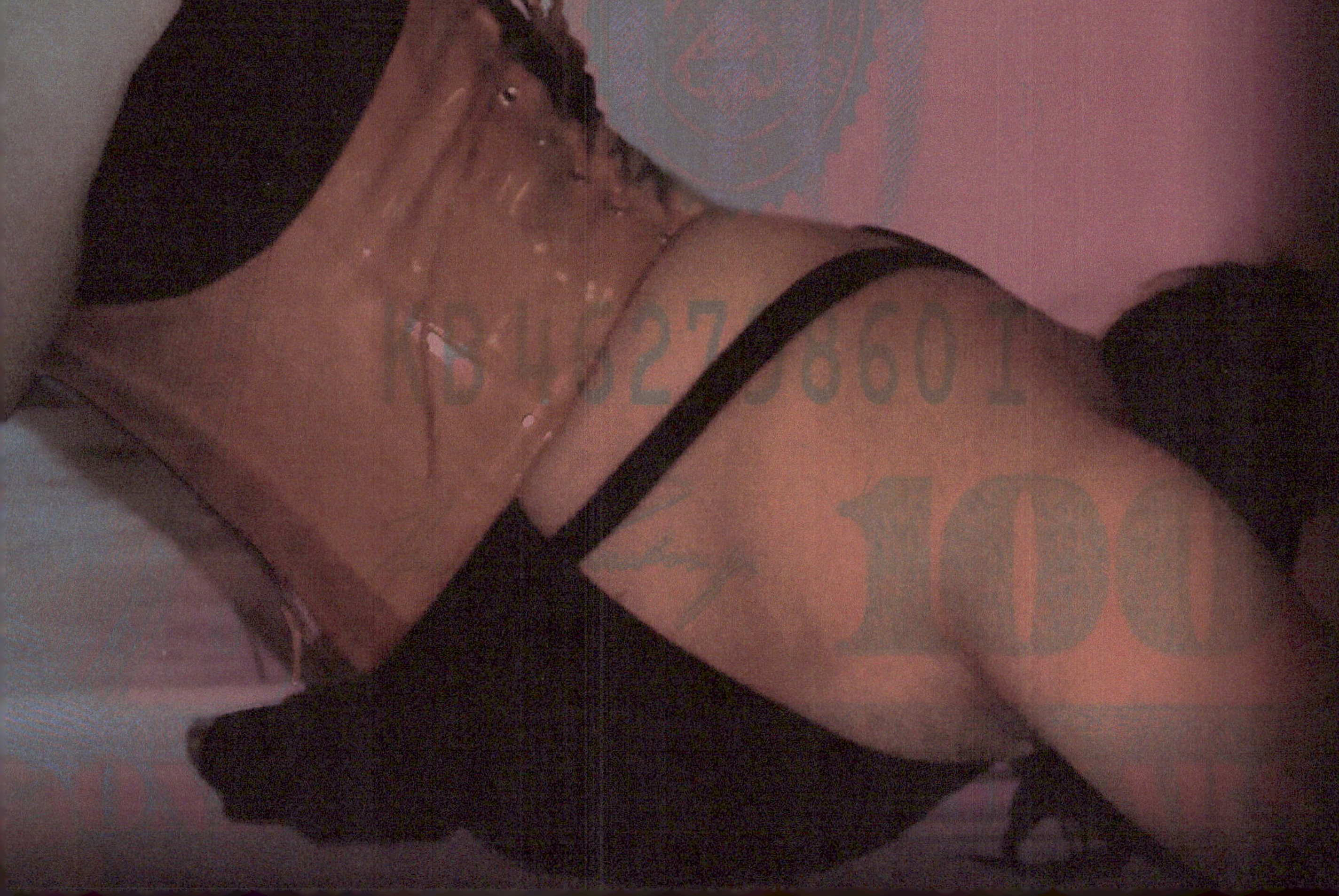

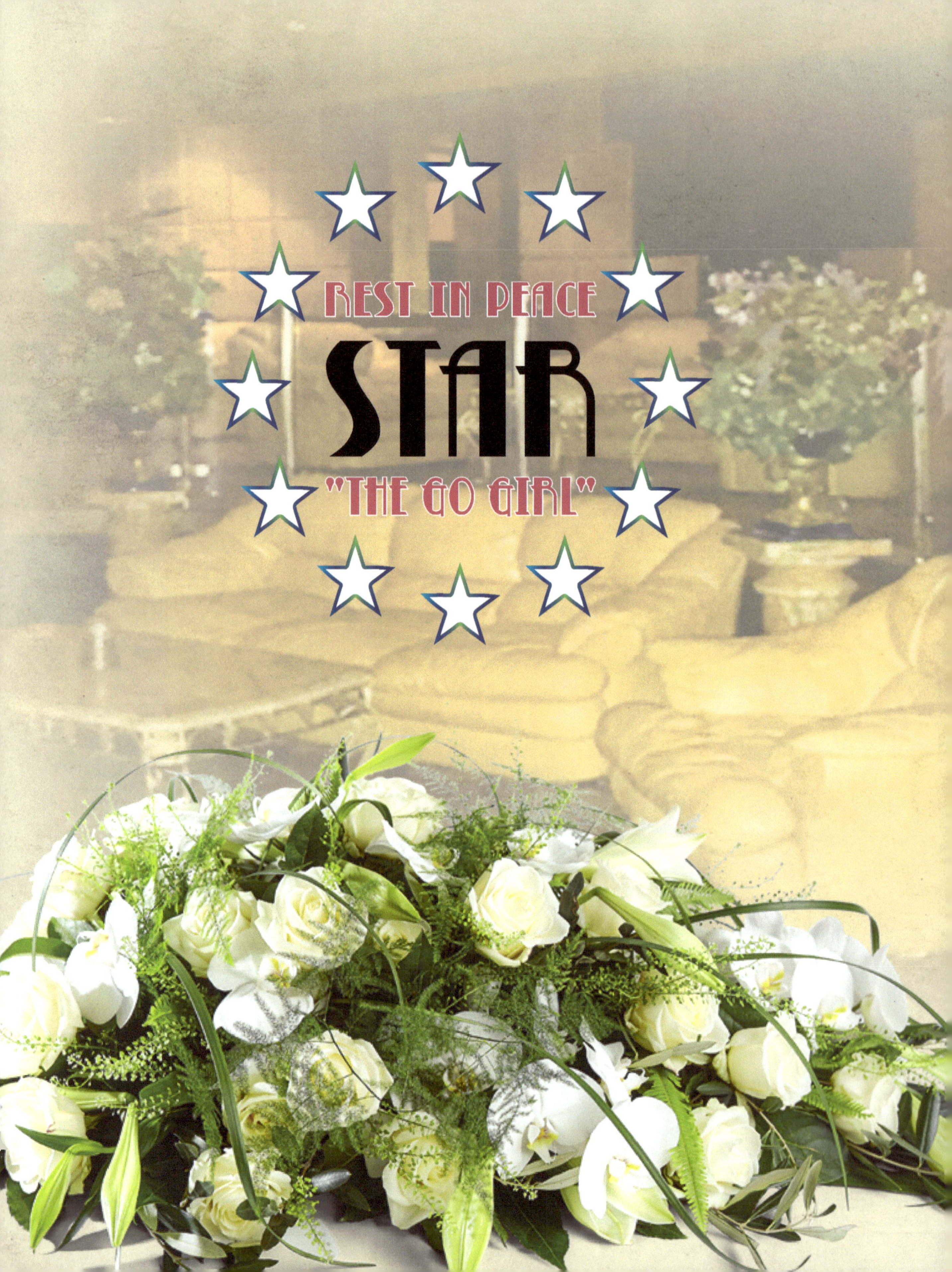
REST IN PEACE
STAR
"THE GO GIRL"

Star and I would steal each other's songs. Sure she was always in drama with the Nikkis and the other girls that lived with them.She was a goofball and a bad bitch hustler before we even knew that was what to call her, society hadn't caught up yet. She'd come on stage, grab the pole, do a single pirouette, and gather a quick crowd. Dark hair and the Italian princess face with a skinny petite frame and monkey toe in shoes that didn't fit. She would ask every stage patron for a room flat out first question, then physically take all the money they had out regardless of their answer. In the time I knew her this was standard. She'd have a wait list for time spent with her and money shame those who only got lap dances. All accounts after I knew her reflected a dark and dangerous time.

Rest well, Star.

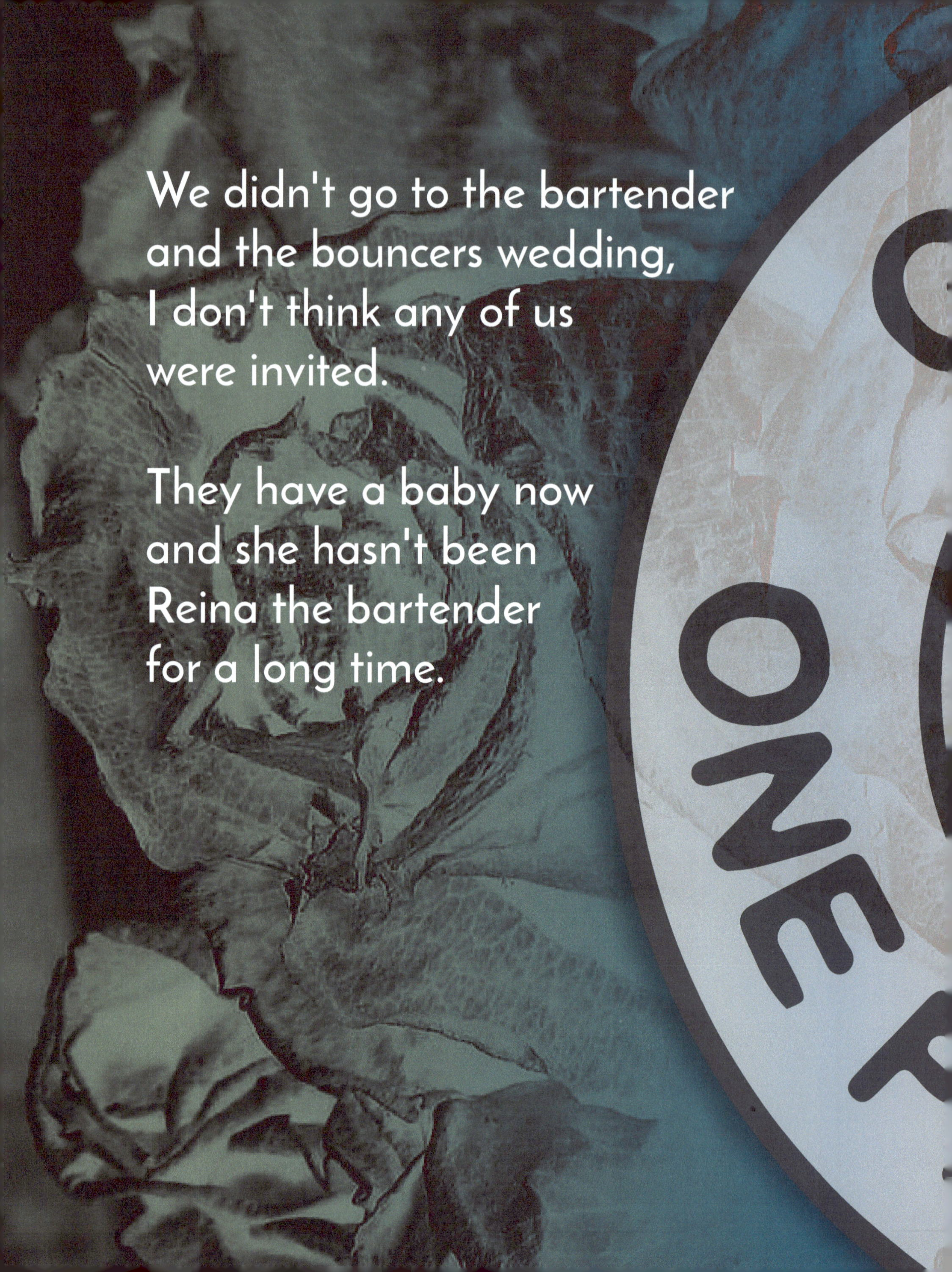
We didn't go to the bartender
and the bouncers wedding,
I don't think any of us
were invited.

They have a baby now
and she hasn't been
Reina the bartender
for a long time.

ONE

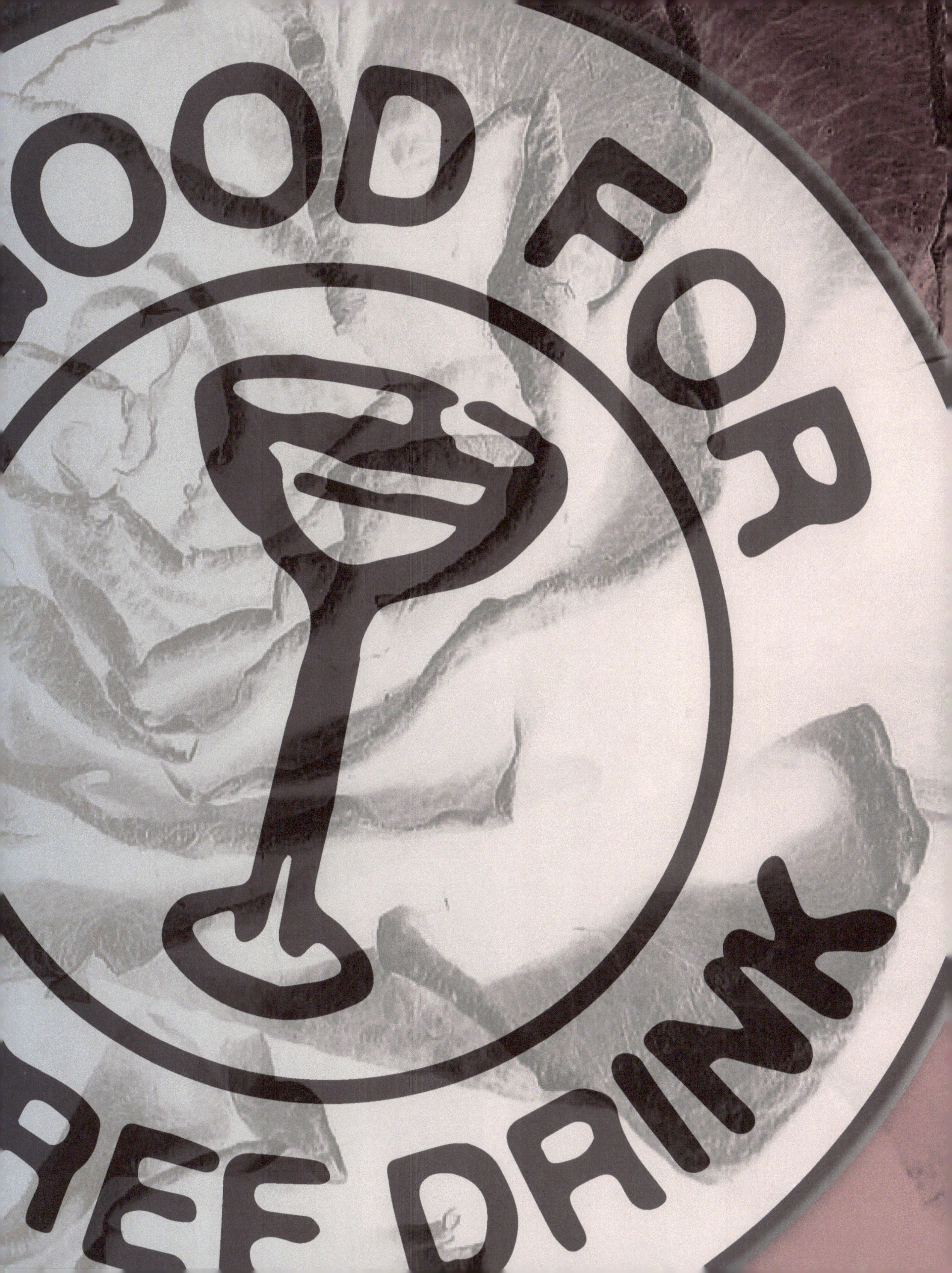
OOD FOR
REE DRINK

Angela brought me into my first club. She was
a trashy girl by all respects. That was intriguing
I guess, she'd out sell the managers' favorites
by a mile.

"Another lapdance for candy?" they ask
sarcastically and clearly offended. But they
hired her.

She would say things, her truths I suppose.

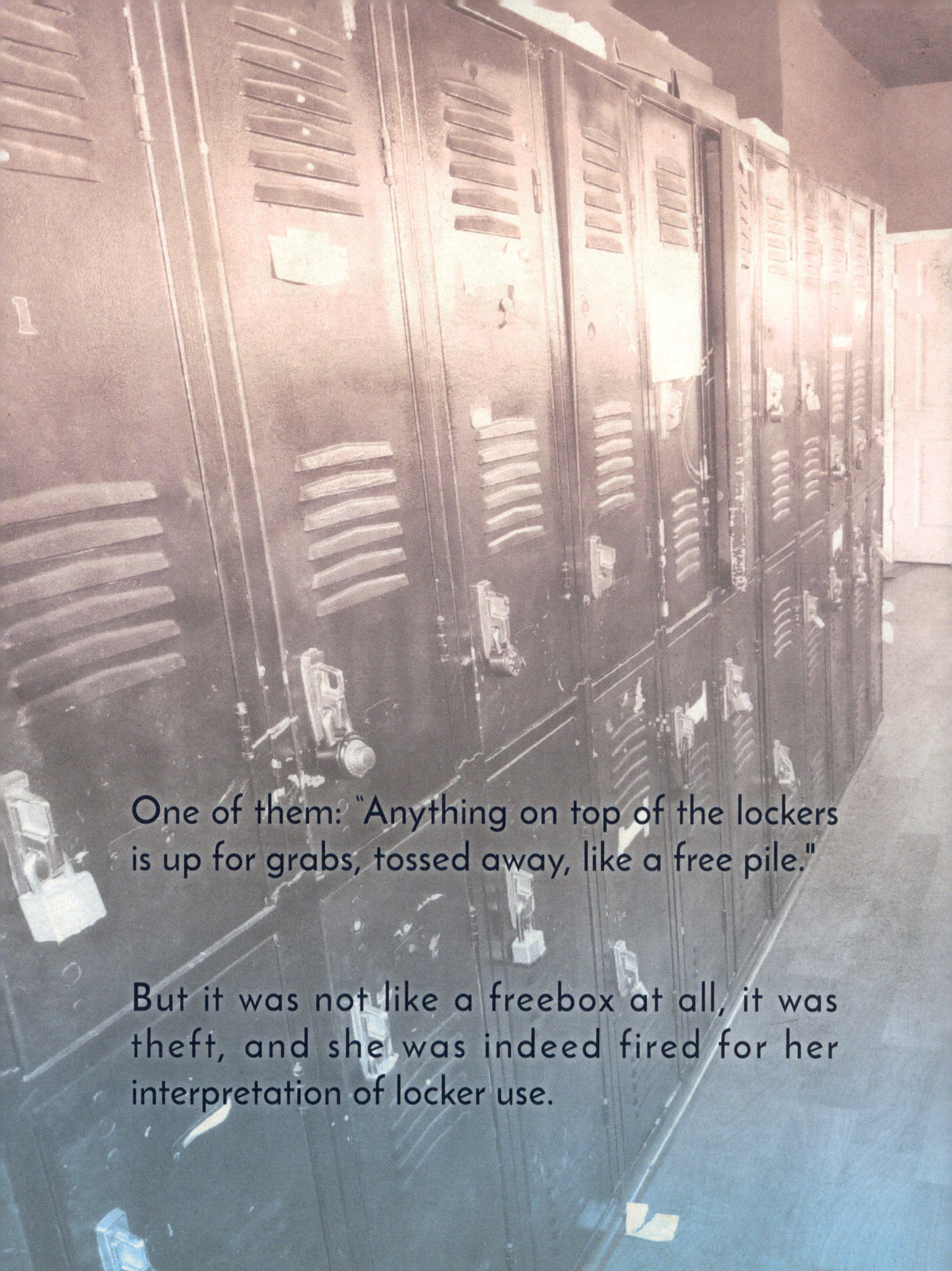

One of them: "Anything on top of the lockers is up for grabs, tossed away, like a free pile."

But it was not like a freebox at all, it was theft, and she was indeed fired for her interpretation of locker use.

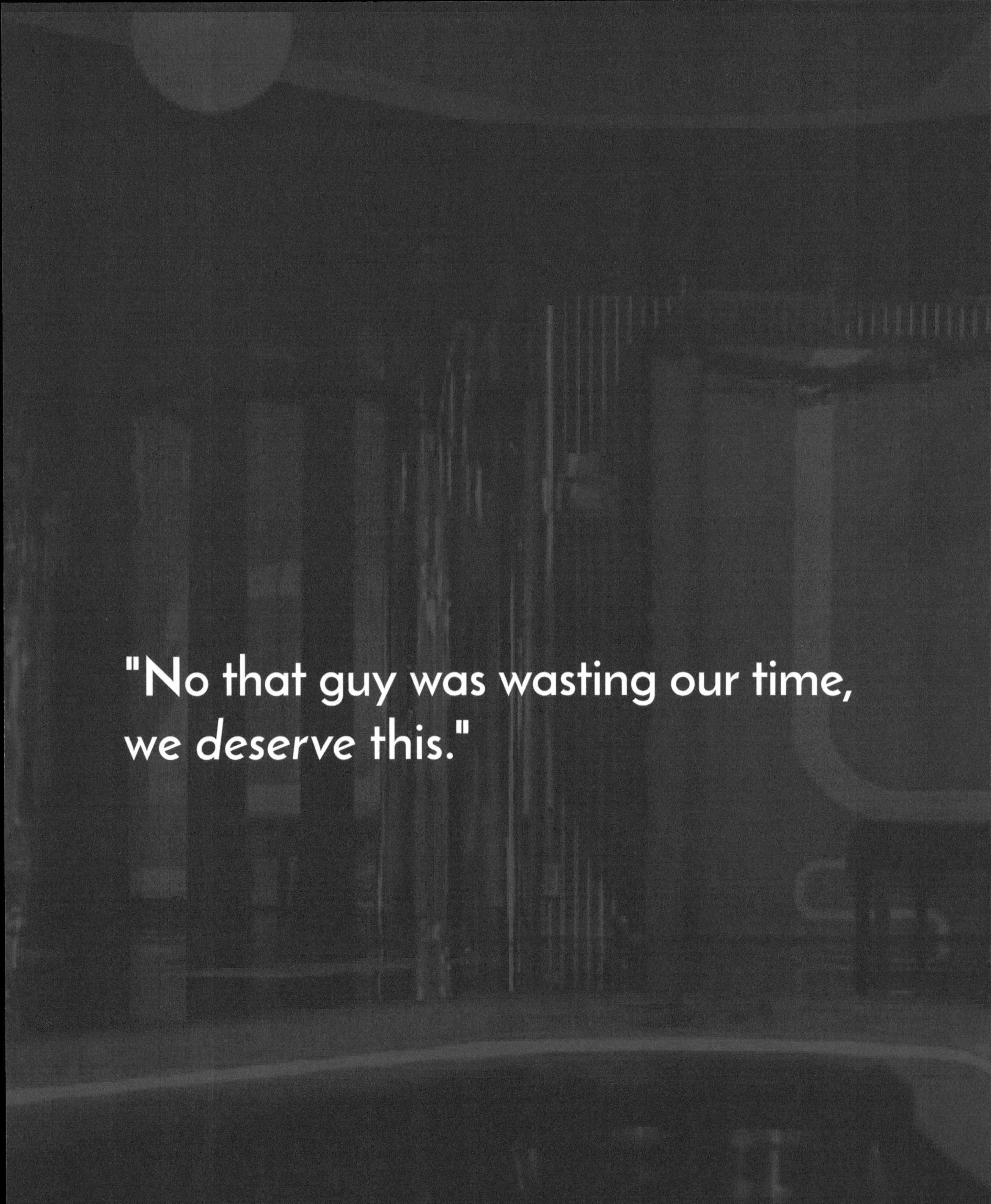

"No that guy was wasting our time,
we *deserve* this."

... on stealing money from a drunk guy and hiding it in her hair.

Authors Note

It's one thing to regurgitate memories, but when I was asked to do this it stopped me dead in my tracks. The truth is it's strange to have context for a whole alternative life you lived after dark. Stepping back into a moment takes nothing but recollection, most of which are humorous and consoling. It's this cognitive part that has no real place. It's still disorienting to play an old stage set in its order in the car years after the moment has passed in a new state and timeline. It may sound odd, but I grew up in that timeline, I learned how to do my makeup and quick ways to do my hair. I painstakingly learned the boundaries of my body and mentality through exacerbation and reprise on a daily basis. But we all did, so I wrote this stuff down. Why? For What? Who cares? Is it important? It's funny how those questions hit you in silly moments of reflection after a decade passed by quietly roaring through 12-hour nights of verbal and physical assault. Or at that moment hiding in the dressing room or bathroom of the club praying you don't lose your job, money, life, or sense of self in this world that shuns you yet demands you arrive before 10, that worships and begs you to be there yet demands submission. The whole industry and game is a mind fuck. We're told that we are scum by the same people who pay thousands of dollars to peer past the curtain and engage. They spit on us under the sun and pay for our time by-the-minute under the moon. Never let your daughter do it, but blow her whole tuition on some girl named "Candy" when you feel insecure.

Watching the news and the industry change shape accordingly has been cringeworthy and a motivator for public and private activism alike. Misconceptions and exaggerations will always occur but the reality is so simple that it's overlooked sometimes. These are people and women living the lives they've been dealt with. Mothers, retail managers, drug addicts, students, sex workers, scholars, and women otherwise existing in several spheres at once. The fact is we see each other, where the world wants to blink anxiously and look away. We see the lady with her kids at Walmart struggling to get groceries with her hair still tied up with a garter from the night before. Or the student in the desk next to you with pole burn and calluses from the shoe straps, because they are almost identical to yours. There is a sisterhood in that. And sometimes as women we forget that the world already wants us to go away, but especially when you're "that kind"

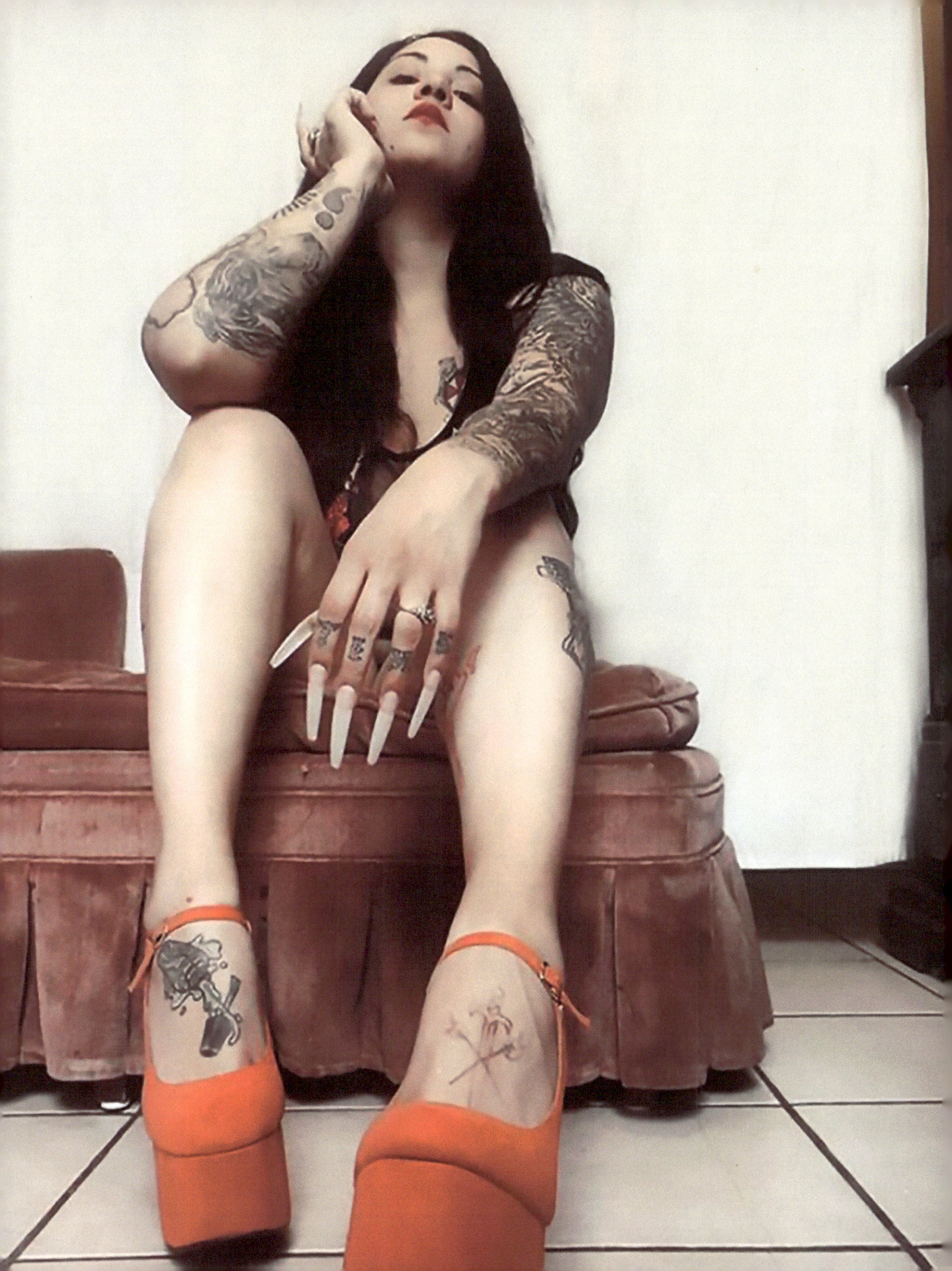

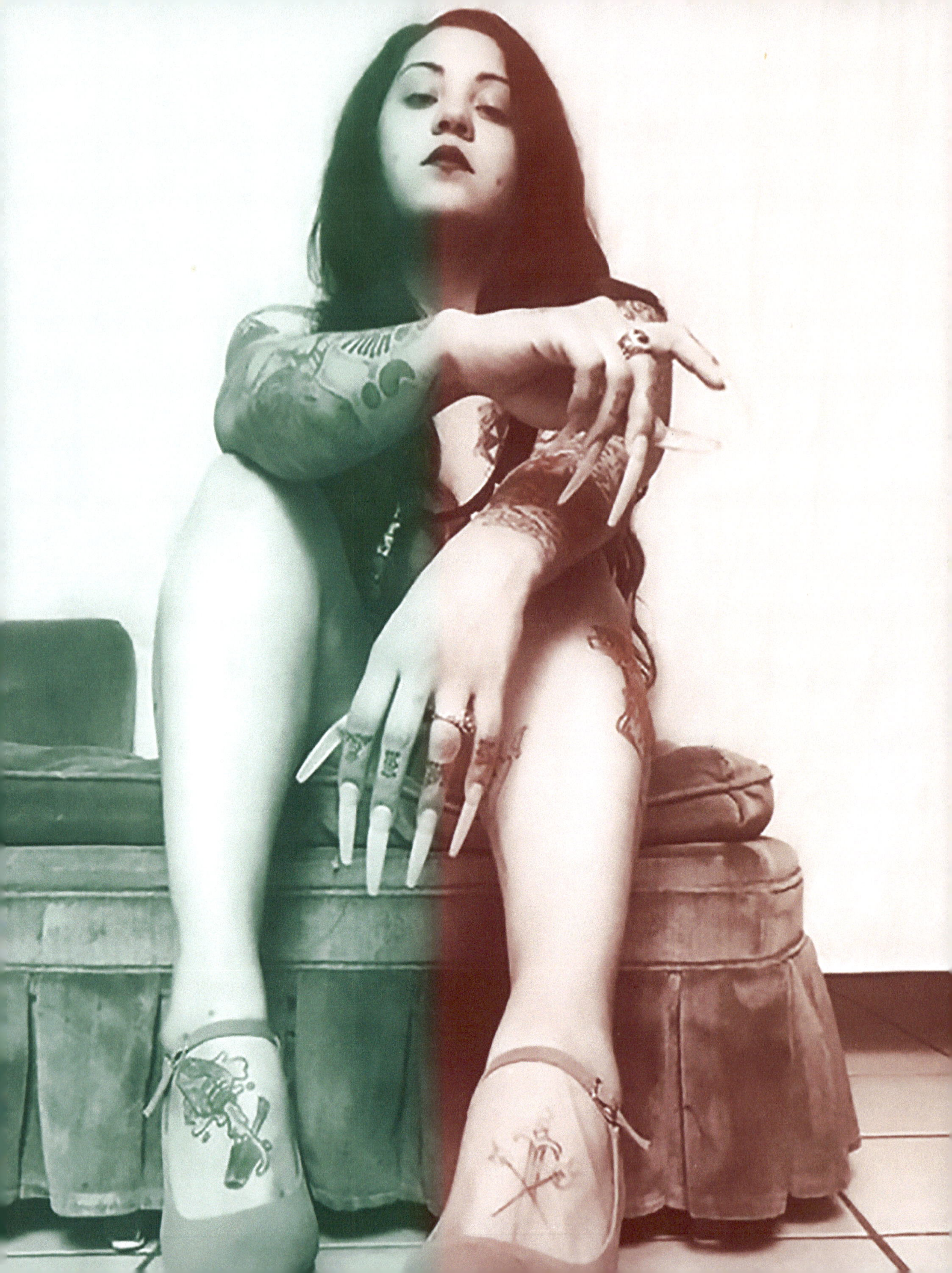

of woman. What we need desperately is to remember that and take back our moments and the implications society tries to peg us with. We need to hold each other up and embrace those little moments that kept us from losing it while society swears we are at the bottom.

Okay so you know, I've been going at this rate and pace for about 10 years now. When you do something like that and then you finally sit down at the end of the day and you start questioning everything that you actually got done, like actually run into so and so or did I remember to go to the Post Office. When you do that with your life something magical happens and we all do it little things people say and do pop right into our mind and they drop you back in time as if nothing ever changed. When you're a stripper for 10 years, life moves on, people move on. But nobody forgets. And in something so wonderfully wild and so painfully deteriorating, everything is exaggerated. There's nothing like watching the news and seeing one of your co-hustlers missing and immediately being reminded of their stage performance. Or seeing somebody out at the grocery store who has evolved just as much as you and saying hi and catching up as if you ever knew each other in real life. As dancers we know it's a different world once you cross those doors and it bleeds out into your daily reality just enough to remind you that it's a very different place. And as more than many of us know it's easy to get caught up in and dissolve into the atmosphere and let this monster of a job take over your life. These reflections are bits of my memory that I love to share that I recall often and with a fondness that I cannot describe to anyone who had never gone through it themselves. These are the people, the persons and personalities and characters of the stories and events, of a person who existed and its own very real alternate reality. They are the shared memories of people still with us and passed on, at the job and in life.

No doubt some of my greatest and best girls are still living their stories and collecting their memories. And these are the stories, the memories that kept my lives in both worlds from crashing. These are some of the strongest most resilient women I have ever met. The most crass situations that build character taught me about life and survival. They are damning and redeeming, they are joyful and yet filled with pain. They are things I am and have shared with the world yet they alienate and personify loneliness. And who fucking cares.

Forever grateful nevertheless.

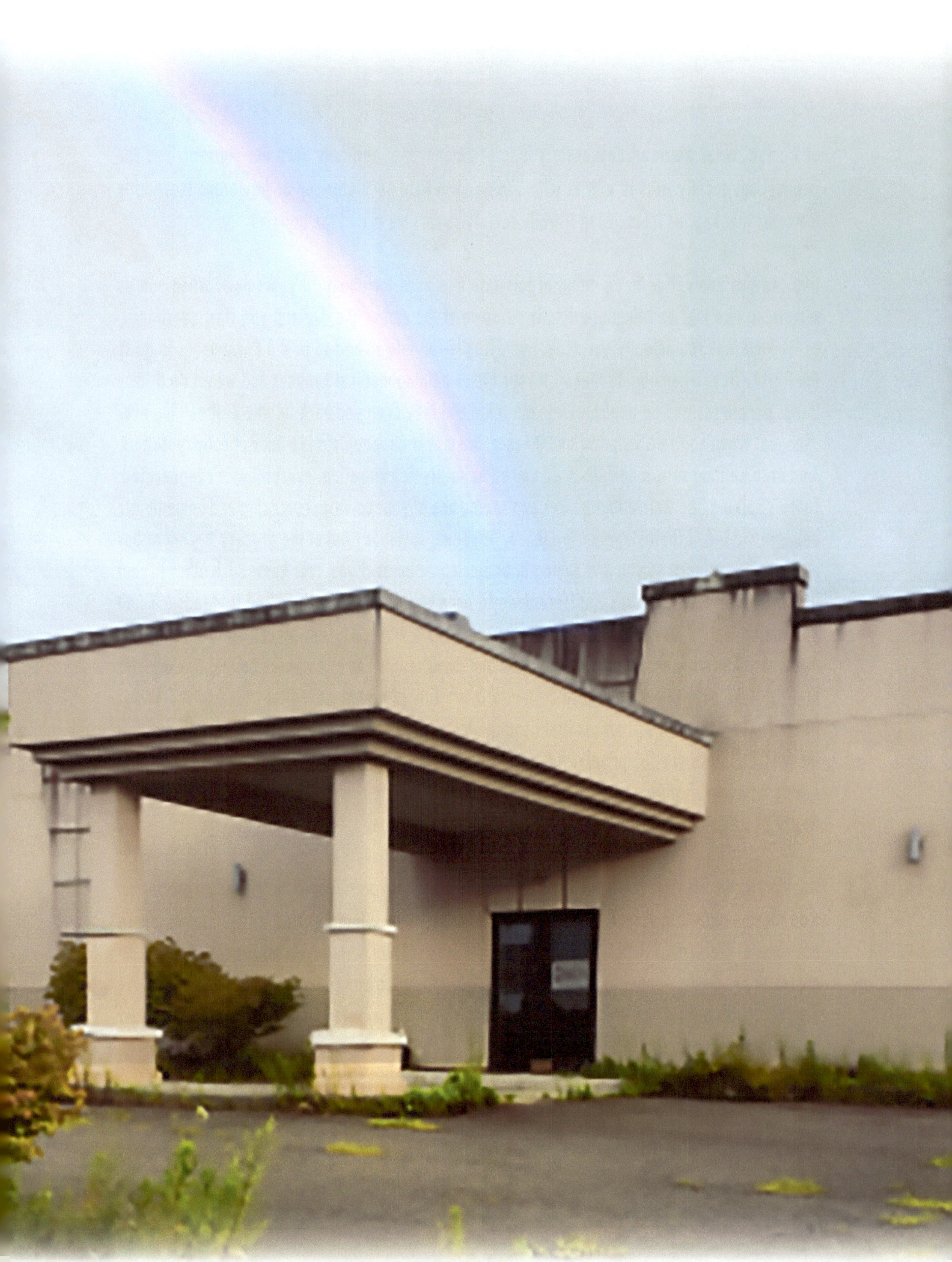